Making SPACE at the Well

Mental Health and the Church

JESSICA YOUNG BROWN, PhD

Foreword by Micah L. McCreary, PhD

D1595317

JUDSON PRESS
PUBLISHERS SINCE 1824
VALLEY FORGE, PA

Making SPACE at the Well: Mental Health and the Church
© 2020 by Judson Press, Valley Forge, PA 19482-0851
All rights reserved.

Interior and cover design by Wendy Ronga, Hampton Design Group.

Library of Congress Cataloging-in-Publication data
Names: Brown, Jessica Young, author. Title: Making space at the well: mental health and the church/Jessica Young Brown, PhD; foreword by Micah L. McCreary, PhD. Description: Valley Forge, PA: Judson Press, 2020. | Includes bibliographical references and index.
Identifiers: LCCN 2019047511 (print) | LCCN 2019047512 (ebook) | ISBN 9780817018115 (paperback) | ISBN 9780817082109 (epub)
Subjects: LCSH: African Americans–Religion. | Mental health–Religious aspects--Christianity. Classification: LCC BR563.N4 B674 2020 (print) | LCC BR563.N4 (ebook) | DDC 261.8/32208996073–dc23
LC record available at https://lccn.loc.gov/2019047511 LC ebook record available at https://lccn.loc.gov/2019047512 Cataloging-in-Publication Data available upon request. Contact cip@judsonpress.com.

Printed in the U.S.A.
First printing, 2020.

To the memory of my father, Barry Terence Young.
His journey shaped my passions and purpose in ways
that he was never fully able to comprehend.
His contagious love for the black church
and the people in it is embedded in the
pages that follow. Love always.

And to
my husband, my favorite coach
and ultimate supporter;
my mother, my model for life and ministry;
my kids, my inspiration to do awesome things;
and Lakisha, my sistafriend and writing partner.

Contents

Foreword

Ministry for Mental Health in the Black Church

Almost 35 years ago, my best friend and colleague, the Reverend Barry Terence Young of Richmond, Virginia, came to me privately and shared that his daughter, Jessica Jeana Young (i.e., Dr. Jessica Young Brown), wanted to be a psychologist. He asked if I would mentor her in the profession. I look back on that conversation as life-changing—for Jessica and for me. Little did the future Dr. Brown and I know the journey we would travel together as mentor-mentee, student-professor, colleagues, and family.

Many church-based mental health professionals, pastoral counselors, clergy, and caring lay leaders frequently hear, "I don't want to meet with a professional counselor." Or, "Professional counselors don't know God and are not saved." This amazing book by Dr. Jessica Young Brown, *Making SPACE at the Well*, addresses in a clear, practical, and detailed approach this and many other mental health-related matters affecting the black church.

Too often, leaders in the church, and in the black church specifically, worry about recommending or accessing mental health professionals because they have been taught that "believers" only need the Word, fasting, and prayer. In this book, Dr. Brown challenges readers to expand their idea of what God can do, particularly through the work of pastoral care and counseling with a trained mental health professional. Beginning with a differentiation between "ministry for mental health" and "mental health ministry" that is enlightening and 100 percent on point, Dr. Brown goes on to discuss mental health stigma, examining this phenomenon from a historical perspective. She gives clear examples of how to overcome the stigmas associated with seeking mental health care and presents techniques and systems to help address negative stereotypes and cultural vulnerabilities, including strategies for community-wide interventions. As a Licensed Clinical Psychologist and Assistant Professor of Counseling and Practical Theology at the Samuel DeWitt Proctor School of Theology at Virginia Union University, Dr. Brown stands, teaches, practices, and consults at "the intersection of mental health and faith." Her status gives her critically strategic and structural positioning that is necessary for healing in the Christian community. Dr. Brown is a superstar in our profession and her words in this book reflect the brilliance and expertise she brings to both the classroom and the clinic.

Equally powerful is the fact that Dr. Brown has grown up as a daughter of the black church. Her family—grandparents, parents, uncles, cousins, and godparents—were and are leaders in the black church. Dr. Brown writes as a member of the community, and as a woman of God who understands the subtle nuances of mental health concerns in the black church. She has a deep and abiding love, admiration, and respect for the black church. She understands its formation, challenges, and difficulties. She also celebrates its victories, resilience, and healing abilities.

In this book, Dr. Brown offers case studies, examples, applications, best practices, and simple steps that improve relationships and promote healing. Her summary of cultural issues at the conclusion of each chapter is incisive and thought-provoking. She couches her discussions about healthy relationships within the biblical metaphor of the village well, incorporating clinical insights into helpful everyday conversations. Dr. Brown also provides instruction about how to build a referral list and guidance on when members of the church community would do well to make a referral.

As a practitioner with 30 years of pastoral experience and more than 20 years of psychological and university experience, I highly recommend this book to all who love the church and its people. I am confident that *Making SPACE at the Well* is a resource desperately needed by numerous congregations and denominations—particularly historically black faith communities. Every church should own a copy of this book! The pastor's library will be enhanced, and pastoral care practices will be improved by reading it and acting upon its offerings.

—Rev. Micah L. McCreary, PhD
President
New Brunswick Theological Seminary

Introduction

Ministry for Mental Health in the Black Church

As black Americans, and particularly as black church folks, we hold secrets about our mental and emotional troubles. Families make silent pacts to "keep our business private." We develop code words to cover up psychotic breaks, suicides, and manic episodes. We say family members are "not feeling well" when really they haven't been able to get out of their beds for weeks due to deep depression. We call suicides "accidents" to avoid the shame of admitting that a family member did not feel life was worth living. We excuse dysfunctional behaviors, saying, "Oh that's just the way they are," rather than holding people accountable for seeking out help and becoming well. As family members drink themselves into a stupor, we look the other way rather than acknowledging the trauma they are working so hard to forget. And while we do these things, people suffer silently, believing they are somehow unfit for full membership in the kingdom even though their circumstances are beyond their control. People hold in their scariest and most painful experiences; they tell us they are okay when they are not; and—this is the most devastating part—they don't get better because healing requires that they acknowledge their woundedness. Jesus said that he came so that they "may have life, and that they may have it more abundantly" (John 10:10). For Christians, living abundantly means being able to bring the fullness of ourselves into places of worship and being completely honest about the wholeness of ourselves, both triumphs and struggles.

This book is for the black church. It is for pastors, ministers, and lay leaders, and everyone in the pew. The goal of this book is to provide a blueprint for developing a ministry that is supportive of the mental health of the people in a black church. At this point, you may be thinking, *But my church can't have a mental health ministry because [insert limitation here]*. Maybe you believe your church is too small, or you don't have the "right" people, or you don't have enough money. I firmly believe that while the actions won't all look the same, every church has the capacity to minister to the mental and emotional needs of people in the congregation and in the community. This book is not about creating a certain type of mental health ministry. It is about doing an inventory of your church and ensuring that people can bring all of themselves, including their mental and emotional burdens, into your place of worship.

The ultimate goal is a pastoral care practice that is inclusive of *everyone*. Pastoral care is essentially all the ways we show love in the church. In the black church in particular, there are some behaviors that we can easily fit into this category: attending the funeral of a family member or a parishioner, sharing the joy of a newly married couple, providing a hug or a kind word to someone you haven't seen in a while, providing some food for a person recovering from a surgery, or visiting an ill member in the hospital. But what happens when you find out a member is hospitalized in a psychiatric facility, or when you learn a fellow choir member has developed a problem with alcohol or drugs? How do you respond when someone has isolated himself from the people he used to connect with at church, and he is no longer answering the phone? What do you do when the daughter of a deaconess has been diagnosed with schizophrenia? What happens when you learn that one of the youth has experienced a sexual assault?

The goal of this book is to give you answers to all of these questions and to some you may not even know you have yet. At our best, the black church is a place of community, of love, of friendship, and of healing. It is a place of gathering where all can have access to the transformative power of a relationship with God Almighty. But for us to do that, we have to make space for everyone at the well of life that is the church. We need space for the sad ones, the worriers, the ones who need medication, the ones who need therapists, and yes, even the "crazy" ones. I should note that my goal is to have you remove that word from your vocabulary by the time you are finished reading this book. Here we are working from a framework that focuses on mental health rather than mental illness. The rationale behind this choice is simple: mental illness is a broad phrase for a group of diagnoses. Mental health is a state of existence and a life process that we all need to work to maintain and enhance. When we talk about mental health, we're talking about everyone, including the "crazy" ones.

You may be thinking that mental health isn't really an issue for your church. Maybe you can't think of an instance of a serious mental health crisis that has touched the people in your community. This is possible, but it's more likely that you just didn't know about it. Perhaps the family elected not to share what happened because they didn't want to receive *that look*. Perhaps they did share, and they were told just to pray about it and God would make things better. Perhaps they were given some encouraging Scriptures and sent on their way. While praying and providing Scriptures for support are at the heart of the ways we care for people in the church, when we are talking about mental health concerns, *prayer and Scripture are not enough.*

If someone has a diagnosable mental health condition, we cannot pray it away, just as we can't pray away a heart attack or diabetes. We pray, and then we seek the help and support we need. We go to the doctor, make dietary changes, and build exercise into our routine. We even wear red during heart month (February) to encourage people to take care of their hearts! We plan events, go on walks, and encourage everyone to be aware and take action. Unfortunately, we do not put the same effort into prevention and treatment of mental health conditions. The truth is, we most often take a passive stance that sends, at best, a mixed message about whether people can receive support for mental and emotional concerns in the church.

Our language and culture provide for temporary "lapses" in emotional wellness but do not acknowledge the inherent vulnerability in our humanness. That vulnerability makes all of us susceptible to emotional struggles and necessitates our connection with other human beings as a part of the healing process. We become so focused on being Christlike that we negate the humanness that Christ himself embodied in order to save us. We love to forget that Jesus acknowledged his humanness in very real ways—he acknowledged his anger, sadness, and uncertainty, perhaps more authentically than we feel the freedom to do. Jesus' decision to save us gives us the opportunity to live in fullness and frees us from the need to crucify ourselves in order to deserve salvation.

The black Christian church has a complicated and interesting history. During the era of slavery in the United States, Christianity was used as a rationale for perpetuating the institution of slavery. Africans were forced to deny or hide their cultural practices and religious beliefs and to adhere to Christianity.[1] For centuries they lived as second-class citizens in the Christian church, being relegated to balconies if they were able to sit at all, needing to ask permission to enter and leave the church, and being ignored during church services. Our present-day churches carry remnants of this reality. Many of us have seen a person raise their finger as they tip out of church at a seemingly inopportune time. I am not suggesting that we move away from or forget this history, but we must acknowledge it! It has the potential to shape the way we understand our relationships with both God and the church.

In the resilient way that people of African descent are known for, enslaved people adapted an oppressive Christianity to fit their own needs. Negro spirituals, hymns with traditional Christian content but with the cadence of African cultures, became a way to send covert messages about the possibilities of freedom. Tent meetings and camp-fires became opportunities to combine new Christian teachings with familiar cultural experiences, such as dancing, singing, and communal gatherings. Figures such as Moses and Jesus, who liberated people from oppression in the Bible, became tangible reminders that God could and would free enslaved people from the chains of slavery. Though it had been used as a tool of oppression, Christianity morphed into a symbol of hope for enslaved Africans. Biblical stories reminded them of the saving and sustaining power of a loving God. Prayer and connection with communities of faith became survival strategies in trying and demeaning circumstances.

After 250 years of slavery, enslaved Africans learned of the prospect of freedom. President Abraham Lincoln declared that they would be free beginning on January 1, 1865. God's promises were being realized! And so, on the night of December 31, 1864, they gathered together, sang hymns, danced, praised God, and waited for freedom. While the concept of waiting for the fresh start of a new year had existed in various religious traditions, watch night services took on special meaning for the black church, and they are still held today.[2] Nevertheless, while freedom had come from a legal perspective, the circumstances of black folks did not change dramatically. They were free, but they were still poor, still discriminated against, and not even considered whole people—except in the church. Black churches became a place of solace—formerly enslaved Africans were no longer required to worship with their oppressors, so they began to form churches where they could worship in a style that was culturally relevant, and where they could discuss issues pertinent to the lived experiences of black folks, as well as ways to fight against the prejudice and discrimination they faced on a daily basis.

The black church was a place where strategies were developed to gain and maintain civil rights. It served as an auxiliary education provider to children who attended substandard schools. It provided financial, emotional, and functional support. It also became one of the only places where black people could be important and garner respect. In most of America, black people were relegated to jobs that might now be considered "menial"—sanitation workers, childcare providers, housekeepers, and janitors. Grown people were called by their first names by white children who were taught not to respect their personhood. In sharp contrast, at church they could be important. They could hold leadership positions, wear their "Sunday best," and be called "Mr. and Mrs." In church they could walk with pride and be more than the sum of their previous experiences. Time spent in the church began to serve as a brief escape from the harsh realities of life as a black person in America. Black people could not forget the daily struggle against racism and prejudice, but they could, even if only temporarily, transcend it while in places of worship.

Collateral damage from this "overcoming" process is a pattern of presenting *only* the best of ourselves in church. While it was appropriate to discuss or even bemoan public suffering and struggle in the church, personal trials gradually became pushed away in favor of an outward presentation of strength and valor. Marital concerns were prayed about in silence, and a brave face was put on for Sunday morning worship. People who were heavily abusing substances would "sober up" on Sundays before returning to the vicious cycle on Sunday evenings. Family members who were struggling emotionally were said to have physical ailments and put on the prayer list. The fragility of the status provided by church membership could not be disturbed by the realities of an utterly human life. This was an old, familiar survival strategy. Enslaved Africans who were literally fighting for their lives could not be bothered with their feelings or their relational problems. The only way to make it was to keep going no matter what. Patterns of emotional suppression and denial became embedded in the cultural

DNA of black folks and persisted even though we were "free." What we have not been able to navigate as successfully is what freedom looks and feels like. We carry with us the need to censor and manage ourselves in ways that often end up hurting us more than they help us.

It is through the lens of this very real cultural reality that we return to the issue of mental health in the black church. These cultural patterns of self-denial set the stage for a church that is prepared to provide community support but often struggles with recognizing and responding to the individual personal crises that people might face anytime their difficulties might be seen as "personal failings." The black church is a peculiar institution. So, if we are to adequately address the mental health needs of those who are a part of it, we need a peculiar solution. The model presented here takes into account the very particular cultural experience of the black church along with what research tells us about best practices in mental health prevention and intervention to provide a framework to help black churches fully serve the mental health needs of the entire congregation.

Consider for a moment the image of a well in a biblical community. During the historical period in which many of our biblical stories were occurring, the well was a hub of community activity, and for good reason.[3] This was long before the days of running water, and so daily trips to the well were a necessity. Women would gather there to retrieve the water needed for the day's activities. As they collected their water, they likely shared the day's news, compared menus for the day, and engaged in chitchat. They got their social fix before a hard day's work while also gathering the critical ingredient they needed to get through the day—water. The well, then, served two critical purposes: it was a place of community connection and a source of physical sustenance. Numerous biblical references signify that the well was an important place in the life of the faith community. In the times of Abraham, Isaac, and Jacob, the construction of a well was an indication that people were settling in a place and putting down roots. Wells were named in ways that confirmed and reaffirmed God as the ultimate provider. At our best, the well represents what the church can be—a place where we can all come for sustenance, community, and support.

However, even in Bible times, communal prejudices and misconceptions prevented some people from participating in this important family gathering. Consider the Samaritan woman in John 4. Jesus had been traveling and found himself near a well in Samaria near the middle of the day. Few people came to the well during this time; most came to get their water early in the morning. This Samaritan woman encountered Jesus at the well at the "wrong" time of day, and he asked her for a drink. She quickly reminded him that Jews and Christians should not be mixing. Samaritans were looked down upon by Jews because of cultural differences. Jews and Samaritans had fundamental differences about how God should be worshiped, and this led to a great divide between the communities. The disdain was so great that Jews even refused to use dishes that had been used by Samaritans!

But even in Samaria, where this story takes place, this Samaritan woman still did not come to the well at the time when others were there. She did not feel the freedom to mingle with other members of her community. We will get more into this later, but encountering this woman at noon must have given Jesus an indication right away that she was an outcast.[4] Rather than adhering to the cultural practices of the time, Jesus engaged her in a discussion that changed the way she thought about God and about salvation. He reminded her that the true gift of a relationship with God is water that completely takes away the thirst of a human existence! This gift, connection with the Spirit of God, is what every Christian longs for. But, as long as there are people who don't feel permission to come to the well and gather with community, this precious gift will not be accessible to all of God's children. We will rely heavily on this story throughout the following pages, so it is worth taking a moment to put down this book down and pick up your Bible to read John 4 in its entirety. I want you to have this passage and all its implications at the forefront of your mind as we move forward. As you read, consider the following questions that will guide our time together:

- In what ways did Jesus and the woman test each other?
- What might have been the intentions behind their words and their actions?
- What was Jesus' goal in engaging the woman?
- What was the woman seeking from Jesus?

We will use the Samaritan woman as a model for what it might be like to be in the church but not consistently feel a part of it. From the very beginning of the passage, we see that for reasons we don't totally comprehend yet, she is not fully a member of her community. She is "at home" in Samaria, but she does not feel free to engage with the community in the way others might. She is so impacted by this sense of being ostracized that she gets her water later in the day than everyone else to protect herself from feeling left out, potentially resulting in the loss of much of her morning productivity. This is what happens to people experiencing mental and emotional distress when we don't make space at the well for everyone to come and drink. They may get the bare minimum. They are able to receive enough to survive. But they can't reach their full potential because they don't have the access that everyone else has. This is a problem that we, the church, can solve! All we have to do is make space at the well for everyone.

The model presented in these pages provides concrete strategies for black churches to ensure that every single person in the community of faith finds a space to dig into the deep well of possibilities that is a relationship with God. Along the way we will discuss strategies for incorporating practices into the culture of your particular church that send the message to folks struggling with mental or emotional concerns that they are welcome, supported, loved, and understood. Using the acronym SPACE, we will discuss some practical recommendations that can help you to enhance your pastoral care practices to be more inclusive. In a cohesive church community, everyone has responsibilities for pastoral care, though leaders such as deacons may be the point people for such interactions. Pastoral care happens anytime we offer care, support, and encouragement to people in the community of faith. Each chapter contains some education about the current state of mental health, with particular attention to black people in faith communities. This information is aided by a discussion of a biblical framework to help you live out the recommendations proposed in the chapter. Finally, each chapter ends with a list of Culture Questions to help you evaluate the best ways to live out these values in your church. In addition, the Well Points concluding each chapter will provide you with the most important takeaways from that section.

In chapter 1 we will discuss silencing the stigma—negative attitudes about mental illness that keep people from talking about their concerns or seeking help. Stigma is complicated and engrained in black communities, and it must be addressed fully if people are going to be able to seek healing.

In chapter 2 we tackle the issue of presence and persistence—what it means to be in authentic relationship and allow people to bring their whole selves into the community of faith. Relationships have the power to heal but only when they are real!

Chapter 3 addresses particular applications churches can make and actions churches can take to provide support in the arena of mental health. When we create an environment where people can talk about their concerns, we must be ready to meet the need!

Chapter 4 speaks to some of the fears that stigma perpetuates—cautions that must be taken related to mental health emergency situations, risk management, and understanding the point at which a parishioner needs to be referred to a mental health professional.

Introduction

In chapter 5 we call on the cultural power of testimony; with expression and exhortation, we will explore the language we can use in church to advance the value of care for all persons and invite people into a space where testimony can be shared and the whole community can witness the healing power of God.

The sixth and final chapter is a commissioning of sorts. We will review the prevailing values that can guide your thought process and actions in caring for the whole community.

Now I invite you on a journey to explore how you can make SPACE at the well of your community for everyone to come and drink living water.

Notes

1. Carter Godwin Woodson, *The History of the Negro Church* (Washington, DC: Associated Publishers, 1979), 23–39.

2. New York Public Library and Schomburg Center for Research in Black Culture, *The New York Public Library African American Desk Reference* (New York: Wiley & Sons, 1999).

3. Walter Harrelson, *The New Interpreter's Study Bible* (Nashville: Abingdon, 2003), John 4:1–15; Merrill F. Unger, *The New Unger's Bible Dictionary* (Chicago: Moody, 1966), s.v., "well." Unger discusses both the functional aspects of the well in community and its figurative symbolism as a metaphor for spiritual renewal and sustenance.

4. David Guzik, "John Chapter 4," Enduring Word, accessed November 5, 2019, https://enduringword.com/bible-commentary/john-4/.

CHAPTER 1

Silencing the Stigma

We cannot have a thorough conversation about issues of mental health in the black church without talking about stigma. The definition of *stigma*, according to *Merriam-Webster*, is "a mark of shame or discredit."[1] *Stigma* is a term that represents negative attitudes or perceptions people can have about a particular issue that they perceive to be marked by shame. These attitudes encompass feelings about the self as well as others. While stigma is characteristic of a thought process, it is also very connected to behaviors. In the black community, mental health stigma is rampant and powerful. For decades researchers have documented the existence of mental health stigma for black folks and how this can lead us to avoid seeking out mental health services, delay treatment longer than people in other ethnic groups, and discontinue treatment before feeling better.[2]

To have effective ministry for mental health in a black church, we must directly address the phenomenon of stigma and how it impacts our thoughts, perceptions, and behaviors. People with mental and emotional concerns might consider themselves unworthy or might shy away from community membership or leadership positions because of beliefs about themselves as inadequate in some way. Others in the community might perceive those with mental or emotional concerns as dangerous, erratic, or problematic. To fully understand the stigma we face, we must examine it through a historical lens.

Think back to our discussion of the cultural realities of the black church in the introduction. One of the consequences of the church being a place where black folks could have status and be important

1

is that they also picked and chose which parts of themselves were eligible to be presented in places of worship. A strong cultural tradition of keeping family business private controlled what remained hidden. Especially things that were considered "blemishes" would be held close to the chest, sometimes even kept from people within the family! (Ever learn something about a family member and wondered how you never found out about it before?) Combine this with the very real distrust of medical professionals that black communities experienced. This distrust was not misplaced paranoia. It was a reasonable reaction to real misuse and abuse at the hands of the medical establishment.

Take, for example, the Tuskegee Syphilis Study. From 1932 to 1972, the United States Department of Health, Education, and Welfare conducted an experiment in Macon County, Alabama, to study the effects of untreated syphilis.[3] This study was composed entirely of African American men. When a treatment, penicillin, became available for the condition in the 1950s, these men were not provided with treatment; instead, they were left to deal with the consequences of a completely treatable disease. In many cases, the men were actually under the false impression that they were being treated. Understandably, this case, among others, set the stage for a deep-seated cultural belief that medical professionals did not have the best interests of black folks in mind.

While this mistrust is rooted in history, it is perpetuated in modernity. Only in recent decades has cultural competency become a part of training programs for medical and mental health professionals.[4] Before this time, even when white doctors would see black patients, there was no guarantee that they would be understanding and respectful of the cultural experiences that impacted the way blacks moved in the world and of how black people understood their own health and responded to treatment.

Because of systemic racism and exclusion from educational systems, a shortage of black professionals in medical and mental

2

health systems still exists. For people who need to see a person who looks like them in order to feel comfortable, this lack of black professionals creates an immediate barrier to treatment. Cultural competency continues to be a problem in medical professions and has very real consequences for the health of black folks. I cannot tell you how many times a person has come to me for mental health treatment and said they went to a medical professional and felt misunderstood.

While this reality is slowly changing, history and tradition can make it hard to take the first step and go to counseling. Thankfully, ever-increasing numbers of African Americans are going into the mental health and medical fields. Finding professionals who look like us and understand our reality is becoming easier and easier. What seems to be changing more slowly than the actual number of professionals available is our willingness to seek out help when we need it. Black folks are often seen as wearing strength as a badge of honor. Seeming to be equipped to overcome anything has become a part of our cultural heritage! While this can certainly be seen as a positive attribute, it can make it difficult for us to admit when we are not doing well. We worry that family members might look at us differently if they see us struggling or that they might send implicit or explicit messages that we should just get over it. We might feel judgment from people who love us when we seem somehow incapable of managing our lives.

One consequence of keeping our personal struggles hidden is that we black folks are often unaware of our family history related to mental health. Discussing our mental health is important because unless we do, we may not have a good estimate of our genetic risk for developing certain disorders. For instance, if I know I have a family history of high blood pressure, I can take preemptive measures, such as being careful about salt intake, committing more fully to an exercise routine, and scheduling regular medical checkups. However, if family members don't talk about mental health concerns, I'm not able to take this same preventive approach with my mental wellness.

To the cultural factors that perpetuate stigma, add the fact that black people are disproportionately affected by poverty. This means that we are less likely to have health-care coverage, less likely to have the disposable income to pay the additional copayments that might go along with going to therapy, and less likely to live in communities where mental health resources are easily accessible.[5] The combination of cultural and financial barriers to treatment becomes a heavy burden to bear. Finding reasons *not* to seek help can be easy, as can finding reasons to try to manage it yourself.

We see the impact of this combination of factors when we look at the mental health statistics for members of the black community. While black Americans experience mental health symptoms at the same rate as other cultural groups (about 20 percent of the population), they are much less likely to seek treatment for mental health symptoms.[6] As discussed above, when we seek out treatment, we do so only after dealing with symptoms on our own for much longer, and we are much more likely to end treatment before the symptoms are gone or are at a manageable level.

These facts paint a picture of stigma that is complex, deep-seated, and engrained in the psyche of black folks. In fact, it is embedded in our casual language: "Black folks don't go to therapy—we pray!"

For many of us, praying was our only hope for getting better. We take literally the passage that invites us to "cast all our cares" on Jesus (see 1 Peter 5:7). Our belief in an omnipotent Savior has led us to put all of our eggs in the proverbial basket of faith. For decades pastors have functioned as spiritual leaders and pseudo–mental health professionals, attempting to help people to be both spiritually and emotionally well. They have been our secret keepers, dispensers of advice and sound counsel, marriage counselors, and intercessors. This tradition is strongly held and reinforced in our religious communities, even seeming to feel, in some ways, a part of our cultural and spiritual DNA. Nevertheless, this strongly held tradition need not stop us from combating and silencing stigma. While pastors and ministers are excellent resources, they are not trained as mental health professionals; they are trained as spiritual leaders. Many pastors want to help their parishioners but feel ill-equipped to manage some of the problems that are brought to them.[7] This leaves a void between the help that people need and the help they are receiving from the church. The problem is not with inadequacy on the part of the church; however, the church must understand its role in the community and use other available resources (for example, mental health professionals). If we are to successfully direct people in need of mental health services to the appropriate professionals, we have to deal with stigma head-on.

A major barrier that prevents people with mental health concerns from getting help is the theological framework that leads us to believe that mental illness is the result of demon possession or some spiritual failing. Let me be clear: I am not saying that demon possession is nonexistent or that it is not a form of spiritual warfare that we battle with as Christians. I am saying that sometimes we, as church folks, see emotional (and even biological) problems as so spiritual that we neglect to address the contributing "earthly" factors. I see this pattern most commonly when we get to the issues of psychosis and suicide, but it is likely to occur when discussing any emotional or mental concern.

Famous psychological theorist Abraham Maslow once said that if all you have is a hammer, everything looks like a nail.[8] A very real possibility is that looking to Jesus as our "all and all" makes it difficult for us to see that our problems have other components besides spiritual ones. Another unfortunate consequence of believing that the root of all our problems is spiritual is that we begin to believe that our struggles are a result of our own sinfulness or some personal failing. While we certainly all have responsibility in working toward our healing, the reality is that many people can't do it alone. If they could, they probably already would have! Take, for instance, a person who has heart disease. While we would certainly pray for that person, we would still encourage them to seek treatment, take medicine as prescribed, maybe even make some lifestyle changes to improve their health. Because a mental health concern is not tangible or concrete in the way a physical ailment might be, we sometimes have a hard time believing the issue is more than just in a person's head or more than the result of their own doing (or undoing). That which is unseen is often misunderstood. When we focus only on the spiritual aspects of mental illness, we do a disservice to people who might be doing their absolute best from day to day. Our responsibility as the church is to help people seek out all available resources.

My father, a lifelong pastor, used to say, "Don't be so heavenly minded that you are no earthly good!" His words remind me that we always have to deal with people in their humanness. The depth and possibilities of our spiritual walk can only be supported by the holistic health of our physical bodies and our relationships. Ultimately, our tendency to overspiritualize mental and emotional concerns may be a reflection of our own sense of inadequacy to address people's needs. When in doubt, we pray. Again, this is not a bad thing, but we shouldn't allow prayer to be the crutch on which we lean when there are other actions we can take as well. The bad news is that our fear and ignorance sometimes keep us from doing all we can do. The good news is that we don't have to stay this way!

There are strategies we as members of faith communities can use to fight against stigma so we can get the help we need. From pastors of churches to lay leaders, our language and attitudes can set the stage for decreasing the impact of stigma. These strategies require that we be intentional in the way we think about our human experience, and that we be transparent in the way we live. Consider for a moment this passage from 2 Corinthians:

> Praise be to the God and Father of our Lord Jesus Christ, the Father of compassion and the God of all comfort, who comforts us in all our troubles, so that we can comfort those in any trouble with the comfort we ourselves receive from God. For just as we share abundantly in the sufferings of Christ, so also our comfort abounds through Christ. If we are distressed, it is for your comfort and salvation; if we are comforted, it is for your comfort, which produces in you patient endurance of the same sufferings we suffer. And our hope for you is firm, because we know that just as you share in our sufferings, so also you share in our comfort. (1:3-7, NIV)

This passage sends a clear message: We all suffer. God sees our suffering, and God responds to our suffering. Some might interpret the beginning of the passage in a way that reaffirms the belief that we go to God *only* when we need help. However, I want to challenge us to expand our view of what God can do. God is big enough both to offer comfort directly and to equip others in the kingdom and in the community to provide the comfort we so desperately need. God can use the people around us to personify comfort. We can be healthy when we commit to being with each other in moments of suffering. When we work to combat stigma, we must normalize those experiences that people tend to keep private. This means sending clear, frequent messages that *we all suffer*. In fact, suffering is a part of what makes us human, and if we let it, suffering can also connect us at a deep level. Our suffering is made manageable, even tender, in community.

This passage also directs our well activity. In our moments of sharing and connection, we are presented with opportunities to bear one another's burdens. It means that when another mother sees sister so-and-so struggling with an unruly child, she goes to the young mother's side and acknowledges that she's been there before. It means that we meet brother such-and-such, who admits to struggling with depression or frustration, with a hug, an empathetic word, and encouragement to talk about what is going on with him without fear of judgment or being shunned. Don't miss the critical message here—the well is only a place of healing if people can get what they need when they show their woundedness! I can't get what I'm searching for if I don't feel comfortable admitting I have a need in the first place.

Healthy activity at the well means that we truly see each other. To *be* the well, we must suspend judgment of those whom we say we love. Stigma is about seeing those we look down upon as "other." Silencing the stigma is about looking at each other and asking, how can we make this community a place for all of us to be well? How can we make space here so that everyone can come and drink? When we see "them" as different and separate from "us," we are able to deny the ways that we are just like them and preserve a facade that keeps us in denial about our own struggles. When we work to silence the stigma, we make a simple declaration: I am you. You are me. We are in this together.

From a psychological perspective, there are two ways to actively silence stigma: *education* and *personal contact.*[9] These two strategies will help to gradually undermine and eliminate some of the myths and stereotypes that reinforce mental health stigma. How do these strategies get played out in the context of black faith communities?

To educate we must talk about the issues that face us. For many black churches, this is an uphill battle because it flies in the face of the cultural tradition of not talking about our places of deepest vulnerability. The level of education depends on the community of which you are a part, but in general the best strategy is to start at the beginning. Assume that people in your church have no knowledge about mental health or mental health concerns. Perhaps you start out with a bulletin board that provides people information about mental health during Mental Health Awareness Month—May.[10] Perhaps you do a Bible study or discussion group that covers instances of mental illness or emotional distress that are found in the Bible (there are plenty!). Perhaps you develop a list of Scripture passages that can help people experiencing emotional distress and make it widely available to the church. Add to this handout information about what mental health is, coping strategies that anyone can practice, and some resources, such as community agencies or a point person in your church who is comfortable having conversations about mental health.

Note that ministry for mental health does not require that you have an "expert" in your church. I am specifically talking about ministry for mental health, not a mental health ministry. While we will talk about specific mental health symptoms, this model is not just about "illness." It is also about establishing an environment where all people feel free to share their mental and emotional experiences, whether mild or severe. And it is about normalizing the symptoms we can all have that are simply a part of our human experience. Ministry for mental health also implies that we won't relegate these actions to one committee in the church. Each person is responsible to create an environment where the faith community is accessible to all. What is most appropriate depends on your church. Some churches have the infrastructure and personnel to have a full-service counseling center of some sort, and others do not. Focus on what your church is reasonably able to do well. All you need is someone who is willing to learn enough to guide people in the right direction. Opening the conversation is half the battle. This book can be a first step in that learning process.

A crucial component of any mental health education is reinforcing the notion that mental health is not just something "those people over there" deal with. Statistics from the Substance Abuse and

Mental Health Services Administration (SAMHSA) from 2017 suggest that about 19 percent of American adults have experienced symptoms consistent with a mental health diagnosis over the past year.[11] That means that in a congregation of 150 people, you can expect around 30 people to have symptoms that meet the criteria for a diagnosable condition. Note, however, that these people might be unlikely to report their symptoms or to actually seek out help.

In addition to people who might meet criteria for a disorder, everyone experiences mental health symptoms at one time or another. This bears repeating: *everyone experiences mental health symptoms!* In the course of being human, we all experience sadness, worry, and frustration. At times any of us can feel overwhelmed, unable to manage the demands of our lives, or unhappy with our relationships. So ministry for mental health is not just about providing support to those who might have a mental health diagnosis. It's about providing resources so that everyone in the congregation can enjoy good mental health.

What comprises good mental health? Being in a state of good mental health includes these components:

- awareness and management of emotions
- healthy and fulfilling relationships
- recognition and management of stress
- a positive sense of self

I list these components rather than providing a detailed definition of mental health because mental health looks different for everyone. The fruit of good mental health is a sense of overall well-being and satisfaction with life, good functioning in relationships at home and at work, and reasonable control of one's emotions and behavior.

While most churches have pastoral care practices in place that help people in times of bereavement, we are not as effective at responding to the everyday challenges that grieving parishioners might face. Times of loss are the times that most churches fully believe they have figured out. While this is often true in the days immediately following the loss, many people who experience a death continue to feel emotionally vulnerable for months after the loss, when the church's attention has shifted to other things. When people don't continue to have appropriate support, bereavement issues can be extended and even complicated, leading to greater emotional distress in the long term.

The tendency to focus on things like death and serious illness in pastoral care activities can leave people feeling that they need to have experienced a "big event" to deserve specialized attention. In actuality, sometimes everyday life just gets to us. Sometimes we can identify a cause, and sometimes we can't. The real work of combating stigma is reframing care as a continual process to which we all have access.

Think about the woman at the well in John 4. Because she was an outcast, she felt as though she couldn't come to the well when the rest of the community did. She was relegated to second-class status—she could get life-sustaining water but missed out on the benefit of communal experience. People today who are struggling emotionally may have a similar experience. They dig into their own spiritual practices, but we don't make space for them to suffer *while* they are in community! The shame and judgment they feel sometimes push them away from the very thing they need in order to be well. In later chapters we will discuss some possible reasons the Samaritan woman was cast out from her community. It is clear here, though, that the effect is that she expected Jesus would also reject her, even though he had given her no reason to believe he would.

This anticipation and planning for rejection from people in your own community is the way stigma operates. Even when no actual word is spoken or deed is done, people can sense that they are not wanted or accepted. The natural human response to being unwanted is to remove yourself. So then, stigma robs us all of the opportunity to connect and help each other heal. Stigma is a poison that can ruin our communities if we let it!

This tendency to move away from others works against the second strategy for limiting the impact of stigma, which is personal contact. The theory behind this strategy is that when we have contact with people whom we deem as "other" in some way, we will eventually see how they are similar to us and note our shared experiences. Ministry for mental health must therefore move toward those people who might be guarded in our community. But remembering that self-care and communal care go hand in hand at the well is important. At the well, when I name my suffering, I expect that others will respond to my suffering in ways that reflect the comfort they have received from God in their own times of suffering. If I can't name my suffering in community at the well, we all lose the opportunity for total healing and transformation to occur! What this leaves us with, then, is the insight that relationships are the key. We will discuss this relational issue more in chapter 2.

Since destigmatizing mental health issues in black congregations is critically important, we need to educate about seeking help when it is warranted in addition to educating about mental health symptoms themselves. This means identifying some black mental health professionals in your area or connecting with organizations that provide mental health advocacy and service to black folks in your community.

Although African Americans are underrepresented in the field of mental health, in most areas you should be able to find several black mental health providers. We must challenge the myth that there is no one to help us. In addition to black providers, mental health graduate programs now actively incorporate cultural competency training so that even if a professional is not black, they can still possess the cultural knowledge and sensitivity to be helpful. A key here is that relationships for referral need to be built *before* there is a need. Often the task of finding and providing community resources to parishioners in need is up to the pastor. However, other people could fulfill this role too; they just need to be willing to sit down and have a conversation with potential mental health providers to be included in a list (we will discuss this more explicitly in chapter 3).

You will likely find people in the church who have both positive and negative experiences with counseling and have a passion for developing a list of providers. You may even find people who have attended workshops or events hosted by professionals whom they found engaging and responsive. Those experiences can be vitally important! In chapter 3 we will discuss the specifics of identifying professionals for your referral list. But for right now, just know that a first goal that a church can have for ministry for mental health is to develop a list of mental health providers and have the list accessible when needed. This takes some work on the front end, but that work is worth it to have the resource available immediately.

Culture Questions

■ What is the "resource reality" in your community? How easily can people access a medical or mental health professional? How easy is it to find a black professional? Have you identified other culturally competent professionals who are equipped to work with black church folks?

■ What is the financial situation of your parishioners? Do you have many people who might be uninsured or underinsured?

■ What is your church population like in terms of their experience with mental health concerns? In the past few years, have any mental health crises or diagnoses surfaced in your congregation? What were they? Have you experienced crisis situations that were responded to publicly, bringing the community's attention to mental health issues? Explain.

■ How does your church leadership tend to respond to "negative" situations? To what extent do people in your church feel supported, understood, and encouraged?

Well Points

■ A term for negative attitudes and beliefs about mental health symptoms and conditions, *stigma* negatively affects everyone.

■ Black Americans are disproportionately impacted by mental health stigma and other cultural factors that reduce mental health help-seeking behaviors.

■ Stigma can be challenged through education and contact.

■ Normalizing mental health symptoms can help people feel more comfortable talking about their concerns.

■ Churches can build and update a list of resources to have available when needed.

Notes

1. *Merriam-Webster*, s.v. "stigma," accessed September 13, 2018, www.merriam-webster.com/dictionary/stigma.

2. Keith Dempsey, S. Kent Butler, and LaTrece Gaither, "Black Churches and Mental Health Professionals: Can This Collaboration Work?" *Journal of Black Studies* 47, no. 1 (2016): 73–87, https://doi.org/10.1177/0021934715613588, for example. Other resources that speak to this phenomenon are numerous.

3. Allan M. Brandt, "Racism and Research: The Case of the Tuskegee Syphilis Study," *Hastings Center Report* 8, no. 9 (1978): 21–29, https://dash.harvard.edu/handle/1/3372911.

4. Joseph R. Betancourt, Alexander R. Green, J. Emilio Carrillo, and Elyse R. Park, "Cultural Competence and Health Care Disparities: Key Perspectives and Trends," *Health Affairs* 24, no. 2 (2005): 499–505.

5. Dempsey et al., "Black Churches and Mental Health Professionals."

6. "Black and African American Communities and Mental Health," *Mental Health America*, last modified November 6, 2013, www.mentalhealthamerica.net/african-american-mental-health.

7. Jessica Young Brown and Micah L. McCreary, "Pastors' Counseling Practices and Perceptions of Mental Health Services," *Journal of Pastoral Care and Counseling* 68, no 1 (2014): 1–14.

8. Abraham H. Maslow, *The Psychology of Science: A Reconnaissance* (New York: Harper and Row, 1974).

9. Chris Kearney and Timothy Trull, *Abnormal Psychology and Life: A Dimensional Approach*, 2nd ed. (Belmont, CA: Cengage Learning, 2015), 16.

10. National Alliance on Mental Illness, "Mental Health Month," NAMI, accessed May 18, 2019. www.nami.org/ mentalhealthmonth.

11. Substance Abuse and Mental Health Services Administration, "2017 NSDUH Annual National Report," SAMHSA, www.samhsa.gov/data/report/ 2017-nsduh-annual-national-report.

CHAPTER 2

Presence and Persistence

The Power of Being in Community

One of the foundational aspects of church is that it is inherently a social community. A wealth of psychological research suggests that churches provide important social and instrumental support to people.[1] From a cultural and historical perspective, the black church has functioned as a "village," just as our geographical communities once did. Churches are places where we gather to celebrate happy moments and to mourn with each other. At our best, churches are places where we see ourselves reflected in other believers and Christ reflected in us. Our church communities can provide powerful resources from a social and emotional perspective. They can provide us with a sense of belonging and a reminder of God's love for us. That capacity is what we all hope for in a church.

Our intention is to make the church a place where everyone can come and be welcome; the reality is that there are times when our human biases and prejudices impact our ability to do this successfully. Where stigma related to mental health concerns exists outside the church walls, it will also exist within the church walls. This reality can lead to negative reactions for folks who may be struggling with mental health concerns.

Imagine Jennifer, a thirty-five-year-old active member who suddenly stops attending church and committee meetings. After a few weeks, a deacon reaches out to her and she responds that she has been feeling down and overwhelmed and has not been able to handle the crowds at church. The deacon responds that he will pray for her, and that he hopes to see her soon. He reminds her that the Lord will never put more on her than she can bear, and that she should press her way to the church.

While the deacon may have had good intentions, this interaction is not a reflection of the best we can do. Too often our interactions stop with prayer. Let me be clear about this: prayer is amazing! It connects us with God; it reminds us of our faith walk; and it changes things! But we must acknowledge that many people in our churches need more than a prayer. They need *prayer and action*. Prayer is an excellent starting step, but often folks who are experiencing anxiety, depression, or another mental health concern have difficulty finding hope solely through their prayer life. This does not mean that they are not faithful enough, or that they have somehow fallen short. It does mean that their mental and emotional state can make it incredibly difficult for them to access the positive aspects of faith.

So, what else could this deacon have done to support Jennifer? To build relationships that persist despite mental health concerns, we need to rethink what it means to be in real relationship in the church. Sometimes our relationships in church are superficial and aren't sufficient for supporting others. To truly reach others, building authentic relationships is essential. Perhaps you're thinking that you don't want to have deep relationships with everyone. Some people are hard to connect with, or maybe you just don't like them. Yet I'm not talking about friendship; I'm talking about a commitment to see and understand people as community members in Christ.

Authentic relationship provides people with the security they need to be honest about what they are experiencing. It also sets the stage for a bond that allows people to receive help and trust the intentions of another. The bottom line is that we cannot be helpful to people with mental health concerns if we don't take the time to get to know one another. This starts with some simple steps. For instance, when is the last time you asked someone how they were

17

and actually stopped to listen to their reply? Or when was the last time you answered that question honestly yourself rather than providing a canned "I'm fine" or "Blessed and highly favored!"? These sayings are not bad, but they can sometimes be a cover for real feelings and experiences. Authentic relationship means investing time and energy in people so that trust can gradually be built. This investment of time can look like genuine interest in a person's life, showing up when they need you to, and being consistent in your interactions.

In my years as a clinical psychologist, I have learned that my first goal with clients must always be to develop an understanding of who they are as individuals. I cannot help them if I don't first learn who they are. This first step sets the foundation for everything we do together, because so much of the process is dependent on the client feeling heard, understood, and supported. I can't be so focused on symptoms that I miss the actual human being sitting right in front of me. When my clients truly feel that I have taken the time to get to know them, they are more motivated to engage in the process and to receive feedback from me even when it might not be what they want to hear. And they are more positively impacted by times when I express to them the progress I've seen them make. Relationship matters!

Authentic relationship requires that we love people unconditionally, and that we stick with them even if they don't want us to. I am not asking you to be the therapist of your fellow church members. In fact, later we will talk explicitly about how that is *not* your job. I am asking you to seek after relationship that invites people to share all of themselves. We won't know who the people are who might be struggling if we don't show ourselves to be trustworthy people who care. Sometimes people will mess up—they might miss a commitment or fail to be the model member you want them to be. Authentic relationship requires that you love them anyway.

In a class I teach, I often make a statement that has become familiar to my students: *Bad behavior is the result of an unmet need.* Often the behaviors that we don't appreciate in churches—those behaviors that cause frustration, anger, and confusion, are really cries for help. Getting beyond the discomfort we are feeling is very difficult if we haven't taken the time to truly get to know people. For instance, it could be easy to be annoyed by Jennifer's "flaking" on committee meetings or waning church attendance. As is often the case, the deacon focuses on fixing those problem behaviors.

I suggest a shift here, to ask a simple question in moments like this: *What might this person need that they are not getting right now?* Love? Support? Reassurance? Validation? This simple question produces a radical shift in the way we respond to others. It invites us into a place of curiosity that can reinforce our desire to treat people the way Christ would. It compels us to ask questions rather than jump to judgments. It calls us to give people the benefit of the doubt before we write them off as being uncommitted, unfocused, or unfaithful. It means that we seek to be what people need, rather than demanding that they do what we want them to do.

People tend to disconnect themselves from the church when they are in distress. Often other Christians respond to this disconnect with a hint of accusation. Their implicit message is, *If your faith was stronger, or if you were more dedicated, you would stay and praise your way through this trial.* While "praise your way through" is a positive message, we need to consider that people may leave because they don't know how to be "broken" in church. Think back to our earlier discussion of some of the cultural realities that lead people to inauthenticity in black churches: when we place high value on being seen a certain way, there are risks—sometimes risks that feel too great—with being vulnerable in church. So maybe what is happening is that many people leave because they do not know how to stay. Furthermore, it is arrogant of us to think that the only way people can maintain their connection with God is to come to *our* church. God is everywhere, even at the home of a member who hasn't been to church in months. Maybe they don't know how to answer questions about why their mood is different or their countenance has changed. Maybe they don't know how to be in church without giving something or working in the church. We tend to make allowances for people who are absent due to physical health conditions. In fact, many churches keep a "sick and shut-in" list that provides information about members who are hospitalized or homebound. While we pray for those folks and it is helpful to do so, we also need to be aware that they may need something more from us. For people who have been active in church, being separated from the community can be depressing and overwhelming. They may crave connection and conversation. Moreover, physical ailments can be emotionally taxing, and they might need functional support, such as help with meals, rides to medical appointments, or even house cleaning.

Imagine the mother of a child with autism who feels completely exhausted with trying to manage behaviors that can be disruptive when children are expected to be quiet in worship. Consider the parents of three small children who can't seem to get everyone clean and dressed at the same time. Think of the elderly member with medical problems who has had three friends die in quick succession. All of these people need us to move toward them. Even when we think we know why someone is absent, that doesn't change the fact that they may need to be reminded that the community still loves them and cares about them.

Here are two key strategies for managing these challenging situations: (1) allow people to leave, and (2) listen when they are in your presence. I know—this is not rocket science! But we don't often employ these strategies. Even if this isn't our intention, we sometimes send the implicit message that if someone steps away for a time, they might as well stay gone. This creates a pressure-filled situation for a person who is already in distress. You could make the argument that seeing the situation in this way is not rational. That may be true, but keep in mind that most people are not rational when they are in emotional distress. Just because a person's thoughts and feelings don't make sense to you doesn't make them any less real.

What would it mean for us to let people leave? Think back to the vignette from the beginning of the chapter. The deacon's first inclination was to tell Jennifer that she needed to come back. While this is a well-intentioned impulse, sometimes people do not feel capable of being in community when they feel overwhelmed. For all the reasons we have been discussing, sometimes we don't feel able to do the things we are "supposed" to do. When we make it seem that the only way people can receive the benefits of church membership is if they actually come to the church *building*, we limit the capacity of what church can do and we make our relationships conditional in nature. Remember, the church is not the building; it's the people. Perhaps you can check in with a member outside of a church event, or even make a visit to their home if they are open to it. What if the explicit communication we sent to people was this: *We understand that you need some time away, and we will be ready to welcome you back when you return. What can we do to support you now?*

Do you see the difference? Imagine how wonderful it would feel to know that no matter the reason you are away, your church family loves, supports, and prays for you! This is what the church is able to accomplish if we allow it to happen.

If we choose to make a commitment to someone in this way, keeping that commitment then becomes imperative. We faithfully check in with people periodically, whether we have seen them recently or not. We reach out at the risk of being pushed away. An exception to this is if the person sets a clear boundary, saying that they don't want to be contacted anymore. If this happens, you should always respect that boundary and leave the person alone.

You may discover, however, that most people cherish and appreciate the fact that you have reached out, because they could not bring themselves to make contact. Often when people are feeling depressed or overwhelmed, they isolate. They might know that isolation is not good for them, but that doesn't change the impulse. We have an opportunity to love people through times when they feel alone and to remind them that they will not lose their place in the community of believers.

We must commit to grant people access to community regardless of their behavior. A value that all people get access to community means we cannot let our judgments, ideas about right and wrong, or even our sense of righteousness cause us to exclude others. Ask yourself, *Do we as a church really believe that people deserve to be here no matter what?*

The second strategy for managing challenging situations is to listen to them. When people are in our presence, we ought to attend to them as if we are sitting with God. The reality is, we are! Each of us is made in God's image, and we are on God's mind constantly. Honor your conversation and interactions with fellow church members as divine appointments. Listen for God in them. Listen for their hurt and pain so that you can acknowledge it and speak directly to it. Express genuine happiness that you get to share space with them! Most of us believe this about each other. We often talk about loving people "with the love of Christ." The truth is, though, that our busyness and the everyday ebb and flow of life cause us to view each other as commonplace and ordinary. We can lose the sense of awe when we are interacting with each other, and even in our worship directed at God. Consider Romans 12:9-16:

> Let love be genuine; hate what is evil, hold fast to what is good; love one another with mutual affection; outdo one another in showing honor. Do not lag in zeal, be ardent in spirit, serve the Lord. Rejoice in hope, be patient in suffer-

ing, persevere in prayer. Contribute to the needs of the saints; extend hospitality to strangers. Bless those who persecute you; bless and do not curse them. Rejoice with those who rejoice, weep with those who weep. Live in harmony with one another; do not be haughty, but associate with the lowly; do not claim to be wiser than you are.

This passage sends a very clear message about the mission of the church. Ultimately, everything we do should center around the value of love. In the context of our relationships, keeping our spiritual fervor means a dogged commitment to love people the way Jesus loved. Jesus communicated his love even with people who were doing the wrong thing. He walked with tax collectors, prostitutes, and people he knew would betray him. That kind of selfless, non-defensive love is sometimes not instinctive for human beings, but it doesn't mean that we shouldn't try. If our goal as Christians is to be like Christ, then we should seek to love the way he did and serve the way he did. He said in John 13:35: "By this everyone will know that you are my disciples, if you have love for one another."

Later in the passage, there is a call to empathy: "Rejoice with those who rejoice; weep with those who weep." Ultimately, this is a call to attempt to understand and respect the perspective and experience of your brother or sister. We might look at their situation and think, *I would not respond to that situation in that way. I wouldn't have had that reaction.* To be like Christ, we must come to the realization that how we might have responded does not matter. Our responsibility in that moment is to sit with and understand what our fellow church member, our brother or sister in Christ, is experiencing. Because they are sad, we are sad. Because they are happy, we experience joy. This goal of empathy gives us the opportunity to send a powerful message: *You are not alone. I hear you and I understand you.*

Ironically, sometimes people feel most alone when they are around other people. The sense that you are not understood by the people you are in relationship with is a distressing and frightening one. It might make us less likely to be open about the kinds of things we are experiencing. It might lower our expectations of others or lead us to anticipate that we won't receive care or support. It might even lead us to be suspicious of others' attempts to be helpful. Our call as Christians is a simple one: love people anyway. Reach out anyway. Let people know you are there, even when they act like they don't want to hear it. Persist in relationship *no matter what*.

The second section of Romans 12:15 offers a final admonition: "Do not be haughty, but associate with the lowly; do not claim to be wiser than you are." In other words, don't think you are better than anyone. Don't fall into the trap of believing there is anyone who is undeserving of a place in the kingdom. In fact, our call as Christians is to associate with (reach out to, support, love) all people, especially those of "low position." Do not imagine that your way of managing stress or handling disappointment is better or nobler than your neighbor's. Don't think that because you happen to be straight and cisgender, you can look down on your fellow believers who identify as LGBTQ. Don't think that because your family relationships are healthy, you don't belong in relationship with someone who struggles with relational trauma or domestic violence. When we release ourselves from the emotional burden of superiority, we free ourselves to engage in authentic relationship. We offer the gift of our loving presence to those who need it most. We become the church in its truest sense.

So what happens at the well when we love people anyway? For one thing, everyone gets access to what they need when they need it. Let's return again to the Samaritan woman and Jesus at the well in John 4. The woman was very aware of her second-class status. In fact, in verse 9 she reminded Jesus of it! "How is it that you, a

Jew, ask a drink of me, a woman of Samaria?" Her scenario was akin to that of the church member who stops coming to church because they feel unworthy or unacceptable in some way. They might be thinking, *Why even go to church, when I don't have myself together?*

Notice what Jesus did—he kept right on talking. He did this even though he knew her inadequacies; he knew her "sin." He knew that she had been married five times and was now living with a man who was not her husband—a serious taboo! This reality did not keep him from offering her the gift of eternal life; nothing restricted her access to salvation, the well of living water. Jesus showed us in this interaction what it means to *love people anyway.* He demonstrated what it means to be persistent in relationship. Nothing should keep us from offering people a chance to drink from the spiritual well—not position, not past mistakes, not mental health status, and not even spiritual maturity. When we make it clear to people that they are welcome no matter what, we open the door for access to God and access to healing.

In practice, persistent presence is something that happens gradually. If your church culture has been a closed environment, you might start with something very basic—building connections. A closed environment is one in which it takes people a long time to be integrated into community because people are reluctant to letting "newbies" in. In churches all over the country, plenty of people come in on Sunday for a two-hour service, never connect with anyone, and then leave and go on about their week. What might it be like for your church to build moments of connection for people beyond the worship experience? How about a coffee hour before worship or a community meal once a month? Maybe making connections looks like special-interest small groups or topical Bible studies where people can bond over common interests.

Because we are creatures of habit, many people sit in the same place in a church from one Sunday to the next. Challenge yourself to take some time to get to know some of the people you sit near in worship. Many churches have a program where established members partner with new members to help them get to know the church. This is something that could be done whenever someone requests it. The strategies are plentiful, and there isn't one right way. What you decide depends on your church and its culture, but remember this: relationship comes first! These opportunities to connect gradually soften people's guard and provide chances to get to know and appreciate each other at a deep level.

Culture Questions

■ How do you identify and reach out to people in your congregation who might be in need?

■ What messages does your church send from the pulpit, in Christian education, and in informal interactions about what you expect of people when they are going through difficulties?

■ How are your church leaders trained to respond when people are in need?

■ How do you work to help church members cultivate meaningful relationships with each other in the life of the church?

■ What are the values in your congregation around relationship and connection?

■ What opportunities do you have for members to connect with each other in authentic ways?

■ What processes do you have in place to stay connected to people who aren't active in the church community?

Well Points

■ Sometimes people in mental or emotional distress find it difficult to connect, but we should try to connect anyway.

■ Persistent relationship happens regardless of whether someone is actually coming to church.

■ People in distress might expect and anticipate rejection, so we must take care to show love and support.

■ Rather than focusing on bad behavior, we must be curious about the possibility of an unmet need that is directing problem behavior.

Note

1. For example, Michael B. Blank, Marcus Mahmood, Jeanne C. Fox, and Thomas Guterbock, "Alternative Mental Health Services: The Role of the Black Church in the South," *American Journal of Public Health* 92, no 10 (October 2002), https://doi.org/10.2105/AJPH.92.10.1668.

CHAPTER 3

Application and Action

Talking Openly about Mental Health and Creating Effective Systems

In Luke 14:28-30 Jesus said,

> For which of you, intending to build a tower, does not first sit down and estimate the cost, to see whether he has enough to complete it? Otherwise, when he has laid a foundation and is not able to finish, all who see it will begin to ridicule him, saying, "This fellow began to build and was not able to finish."

This Scripture speaks to our need to plan for what we desire. If we do things right based on the information in the first two chapters related to stigma and building healthy relationships, a natural outflow of this should be a community that more openly talks about mental health and mental health concerns. When that happens, you need to be ready! So what does readiness look like? Readiness happens at two levels; the first is *conversational*, and the second is *structural*.

Conversational readiness means that people in your church, especially those in leadership, feel prepared to have conversations with people about issues related to mental health. These conversations require that we adequately and graciously express empathy and compassion to those who might be suffering. It means we have a sense of what kinds of things might be helpful to say and what kinds of things might be ultimately unhelpful, despite our best intentions. Conversational readiness means that in moments of sharing, we suspend our own reactions and emotional expressions to keep the attention focused on the person who needs it at the moment. This does not mean that we have to be emotionless robots. It does mean we keep in mind our role as the person being helpful in that moment and ensure that the person who is seeking help gets it.

We need to take a moment here to talk about empathy, which is the ability to identify with and imagine the experience of another. It is the proverbial walk in another person's shoes. When we move with empathy, it changes the way we interact with those who are in need. Empathy causes us to ask an important question before we speak or act: *Will this be helpful?*

I know this seems like a very simple question. But over the course of my time in church, I have found that many of us respond with reflexive words that we have heard before, or perhaps that others have said to us. While this strategy is not inherently bad, being thoughtful about who you are talking to and the details of the situation at hand is important. What might be helpful for one person might not be helpful for another. A canned church response or Christian cliché isn't good enough! This is yet another reminder that relationship comes first! When we know people, we can make a better judgment about what might be helpful. If we don't know people, we err on the side of caution and check to make sure we are providing what they need.

One of the times we are most likely to give these canned church responses is when people are in the midst of grief and bereavement. In the black church, we have lots of words to offer people when they have lost a loved one. Our earnest intention in saying these words is to offer comfort. But sometimes those familiar phrases send the implicit (undercover) message that a person should stop having a normative grief response and instead operate with stoicism and "strength." Here are just a few examples:

"To be absent from the body is to be present with the Lord."
"They are in a better place."
"We don't grieve as those who have no hope."
"God needed another angel."
"Everything happens for a reason. God knows best."

While we intend for these sayings to provide support and encouragement, often people who are in the throes of grief cannot take these well-intended words in stride. When I am burying my mother or father, I don't want them to be in a better place—I want them here with me! If I have lost a child, "Everything happens for a reason" feels like a slap in the face. "God knows best" might be an agitation if I'm angry with God at the moment.

Another situation you might commonly find in your church is a married couple or family going through distress or conflict. Maybe one person in the family comes to you and confides about the trouble they are experiencing. They say they are feeling overwhelmed, stressed, and frustrated. Some common church refrains might be things like these:

"Fake it till you make it!"
"Praise your way through."
"What God put together, let no man put asunder."
"Everything will be alright. Just trust God."

In family crises, the person may need prayer and additional support for serious danger or trouble. Is there violence or abuse in the home? Is everyone physically safe? Is there substance abuse or criminal activity involved? Any of these situations would warrant more intervention, and a reflexive response such as the ones above could shut down a person's attempt to request help.

So what can we say instead? In this chapter I will present some basic principles to help laypeople and church leaders live into the "conversational readiness" that is necessary when we open people up to talk about their mental health concerns. Some simple skills will help us to create an open environment for sharing and to meet people where they are.

The first important skill is groundbreaking: *listening*. It's very simple to think about but not always as easy to live out. In our humanness we are often bogged down by the worries and burdens of our own existence. We sometimes don't have the emotional attention span to listen well to people who want to share with us. For example, imagine you are walking into church and see an acquaintance:

"Hi, Evelyn, how are you doing?"

"I'm fine. How are you?"

"I'm fine, and you?"

Has this ever happened to you? We get into such a conversational habit that we aren't even listening to ourselves! Another variation is that one or both people walk away before they can actually answer the question about how they are. "How are you?" becomes a greeting but not an actual question that requires a response. This is not an indictment, because it happens to all of us from time to time. It is, however, a call to attention. These empty interactions will not serve people who are truly in need. In fact, they will send a frightening implicit message: *People don't really care how I am. They don't have time to find out what's really going on.* If the church is to become the well where people meet God and receive the sustenance they need, we must get off autopilot and work to be more intentional in our interactions with others.

How do we change this dynamic? Stop and listen. Listen without having to immediately formulate a response. Listen in a way that allows the person to feel heard and understood. Active listening involves maintaining eye contact, checking to ensure you are understanding what the person is saying, and possibly even remaining silent and bearing witness to what is being shared. Please notice: this kind of listening changes the goal of conversation.

Often when we hear someone talk about a problem, we immediately move into problem-solving mode. *What can I do to fix this problem or make it go away?* The kind of listening I am suggesting does not have the goal of fixing the problem but of understanding the person and the problem that person is presenting. When our focus changes, our behavior changes.

The Forum for Theological Exploration in Atlanta, Georgia, presents an engaging model for "holy listening," a skill to help create a space where people can bring their full selves into the interaction. "In holy listening, the focus is on the speaker. The listener practices a disciplined posture of care, hospitality, relaxed awareness and attentiveness. This practice creates space for calm abiding with one another, and for the shy soul that longs to be admitted."[1]

This should be our heart's desire in the church! We want our churches to be places where people can bring their joys and their struggles, their vulnerabilities and their strengths. Again, in holy listening, the focus is on the person speaking, and the listener practices an intentional attentiveness to that person's experience and existence. It is listening without a desire to respond but only to understand. It is listening with the awareness that this disclosure is a sacred gift from the speaker to you.

If we truly desire to engage in holy listening, we need to be able to do a quick self-assessment when someone brings a concern or issue to us. I know that if I am emotionally overwhelmed or fatigued in my own life, I might not be able to be present. Perhaps I am running to something urgent and might find myself distracted if I were to stop and listen at that very moment. I am a firm believer that being able to be present with a person sharing their concerns is essential. So, if you feel that for some reason you are unable to do that, stop the person with a comment of this sort: "Sister Jones, I really want to be able to sit with you and hear your concerns, but I have something I'm in the middle of right now. Can you have a seat, and I'll come sit with you in about five minutes?"

If what you are in the middle of cannot be easily resolved and it is best to stop what you are doing and attend to the person, give yourself a moment to transition so that you can truly be *with* the person who is sharing with you. Stop and say a quick prayer to ask God to guide your words and actions. Put down any papers or items that might be in your hands, and shift your gaze and body posture toward the person. Take a seat and have a deep breath before the conversation begins. Holy listening requires all of you—body, mind, and spirit!

So, holy listening provides a relational space where people can share openly and completely. It helps us to gain a fuller, more nuanced understanding of what our fellow believer may need. From this place of deep understanding, we can be more helpful. And holy listening provides a foundation for the next basic skill, which counselors call *reflection*. A reflection is a way of making sure that you truly understand what the person has said and a communication to them that they have been heard. The simplest form of this is a brief repetition or paraphrase of what the person has said. It is imperative that this statement be free from judgment or criticism, as judgment is one of the quickest ways to alienate people. It is also something the church has developed a reputation of dispensing without consequence. Because of this unfortunate reality, people might be expecting your condescension and condemnation. They may be anticipating that somehow they will be blamed for what they have shared with you—something they did wrong or something they neglected to do right. Here you have an opportunity to change the negative narrative some folks have about what church is! While what the person is experiencing *might* be a consequence of a mistake or a misstep, acknowledging that at this particular moment probably won't be helpful, so choose to respond differently. Particularly when we are talking about mental health symptoms, people can't simply control them, change them, or make them go away. If that were possible, they wouldn't need your help!

Here are some examples of unhelpful ways people sometimes respond to someone with a mental health issue:

> "Where is your faith? Don't you believe that God will bring you through?"
> "You can't pray and worry! You can't straddle the fence."
> "That's just the enemy trying to distract you. You need to stay focused."
> "Stop speaking that way over yourself! The power of life and death lies in the tongue!"

Again, these sayings are not inherently unhelpful, but the timing and context might be inappropriate. Despite our good intentions, sometimes these words of "encouragement" end up feeling like rebukes. They send the undercover message that it is somehow the person's fault that they are feeling poorly, or that their faith just isn't strong enough. That message is not true, and it perpetuates the stigma that will block people from getting what they need at the well.

Here are some helpful alternatives that reflect empathy and a real desire to help:

> "I'm so sorry you are struggling right now! I want to pray with you, and then we can sit down and think about some next steps you can take."
> "We all deal with worry sometimes. Let's see if we can find a few Scripture passages about worry. After that, maybe we can talk about finding a counselor for you to talk to who can help you figure things out."
> "You know, sometimes we all need some additional support. Have you thought about talking to your doctor about it?"

Note that each of the helpful examples provided has two components: empathy and resources. This brings me to the last point for conversational readiness and a transition into structural readiness. When we open ourselves up to conversations about mental health in the church, we need to have a structure in place to support those conversations. We need to have ready-made resources at our disposal so we can quickly get people the help they need. Across a variety of disciplines, research indicates that the shorter the time gap between when people ask for help and when they receive it, the more likely they are to follow through. People are most motivated to change and get better during moments of crisis. In other words, *time is of the essence.*

Remember also, from chapter 1, that African Americans are more likely than other ethnic groups to delay seeking treatment or to stop treatment early. Thus it is crucial for us to act quickly and efficiently when people seek out help. Consider that by the time they have mustered up the strength to tell us what is going on, they have fought a hard battle and may be mentally, emotionally, and spiritually exhausted. Whatever ways we can facilitate and streamline the process of receiving help will assist in working to alleviate the pain people are experiencing.

Structural Readiness—Building a Referral List

Let's transition to talking about some of the resources churches might need to have at their disposal. While this is certainly not an exhaustive list, it provides a launching pad for you to think about the kinds of things your particular church community might need. To form a preliminary structure, you first need to identify the essential personnel in your church leadership for engaging in conversations with people with mental health issues. Everyone needs to be prepared, but someone has to be in charge. This could be a deacon, a minister, or some other ministry leader. My suggestion is that this person *not* be the pastor, for a couple of reasons. First, pastors have a lot of responsibilities—they may not be able to provide the level of attention needed for a particular issue because their attention is divided. Second, one of the powerful components of this metaphor of the well is that responsibility of care belongs to the *whole* community, not just one identified person. Whoever this point person is in the church, their responsibility is to make sure that people are getting what they need. They are not the only ones eligible to provide care or the only ones equipped to do so. They operate on an as-needed basis.

A second thing to think about is space. Does your church have a confidential space where people can go for private conversations? The best-case scenario is a private space with comfortable seating that is consistently supplied with tissues (because crying is an acceptable human response!) and the church's master resource list, which we will get to next. Logistically, this best case may not be possible. In that event, have the tissues and resource list easily accessible so that they can be reached quickly when needed. In addition, you can have a sign that can be quickly hung on the door of a classroom or office to let others know that a private conversation is occurring.

Related to the issue of space is the question of the process by which people can ask for help. This process will be very dependent on the size and practices of your church. In some churches a person can walk up to a minister or ministry leader and let them know what they are dealing with. My hope is that this is a possibility and a practice in all churches! In other churches there might also be a more formal process that involves filling out a form, sending an email, or making a phone call. These processes are perfectly fine, but they should be clearly articulated and readily available so people know how to ask for help. If your church uses a printed bulletin or has a digital form of announcements, regularly clarify what the process is for seeking support so people don't have to wonder. If there is a dedicated space for pastoral care or getting in touch with leadership, post the process there so it is easily accessible.

No matter the size of the church or nature of the process, a couple of things must be considered. First, tracking requests for help and the way they are resolved is useful. This process needs to be confidential and might be managed by a member of the deacon ministry, health ministry, or congregational care ministry, if they exist. In some instances, once the person's request or issue has been resolved, their name might be removed from the record to protect their confidentiality. In other situations, it might be helpful to keep track of repeated requests for the same type of support from a member (particularly around substance use or serious mental health concerns). Whenever we can help people while maintaining their confidentiality, we should do that. This tracking process helps the church to get an evolving understanding of the needs in the church and what resources might have to be put into place to ensure the church is being as helpful as possible.

Second, whatever processes are in place should not present an undue burden to the persons who are seeking help. Asking for help is hard! We don't want to make the structure any more complicated than it needs to be. Getting a counseling referral shouldn't take conversations with four or five different people. Nor should someone who reaches out have to wait two to three weeks for a response to their call or correspondence. Keep it simple—and quick!

Now we can transition to the services and agencies you might need on a resource list. My suggestion is a general but comprehensive list of the possible resources people might need:

- individual therapists (social workers, professional counselors, marriage and family therapists, psychologists)
- psychiatrists or nurse practitioners
- community health care or mental health care organizations
- social service agencies
- hotlines for suicide and "warm lines" for people who are not suicidal but are in emotional distress
- crisis intervention

■ substance abuse support groups
■ domestic violence support groups and emergency shelters

Developing this list will likely require diligent research on the part of one or more people. In terms of therapists, my recommendation is that for every fifty people on your church membership roll, you should have at least one therapist identified to whom you can refer members. This should be a referral you can make with trust and confidence. Thus the point person will need to do some legwork. Consider the cultural realities of your congregants and anticipate the types of needs they might have in a mental health provider: counseling for couples, substance abuse, general mental health concerns, work-related stress, caregiver burnout, and so on. Set up a fifteen-minute consultation with the therapist with some questions ready. Most therapists will be happy to have a brief conversation with you. Ask them directly if they are willing to be included on a referral list for your church. Here are the types of things you might want to ask a professional:

■ How do you understand clients' needs and help them meet their goals?
■ How would you help a client with Christian beliefs incorporate these beliefs into their treatment? What special considerations do you think about with Christian clients?
■ How do you help clients understand how culture impacts their mental health symptoms and daily experience?
■ Who is your ideal client?

These are just some examples. The goal is to get a sense of the provider's ability to understand and relate to the particularities of the way Christians, specifically black Christians, understand and deal with mental health concerns in a way that is realistic and affirming. If the therapist struggles with answering these questions, they may not be a good fit for your congregation. Another way to identify providers who might be a good fit is through word-of-mouth recommendations from members or others who have had positive experiences with a certain provider. Consider having an anonymous method for members and leaders to provide contact information for therapists whom they have found helpful.

The goal is that when you get to the point of making a referral, the person in need won't feel like you are leaving them to fend for themselves. I call this process the "transference of trust." People seek help in their faith communities because they have a strong belief that the people in the church have their best interests at heart, and that they can get the help they need. When you refer a member to an outside mental health provider or social service agency, you want to be able to transfer that trust from you to whoever that outside person is. This means being able to say confidently and truthfully that you believe in the counselor's ability to be helpful. It also means that you do more than throw a business card at someone and walk away. Perhaps you offer to sit with the member while they make a call, or offer particulars about why you think the mental health professional would be a good fit for them.

A good practice is to check in within a week or two to ensure the member has at least made a call. Making a referral to an outside resource does not absolve you of responsibility; it just means you move into a different role: one of pastoral care. You check in periodically to see how the member is doing, pray for them, and help them to make sense of the process they are going through. You now move into a role as an accountability person to ensure that the congregant commits to the process of counseling and focuses their attention on getting better.

Building a referral list is an ongoing process, and that is one of the reasons why I suggest using some form of tracking system. As your congregation grows and develops, people's needs will adjust as the membership changes, and social issues shift. You may end up having resources for substance abuse, trauma survival, domestic violence, veterans issues, homelessness, joblessness, and the list goes on. In addition to traditional outpatient care, having a list of crisis lines that people can call in case of an emergency is helpful (more about this in the next chapter). A church that is not able to understand and address the social, cultural, and financial realities of its members cannot possibly be a well! While the focus of this book is people's mental health concerns, understand that mental health is just one piece of the larger constellation of factors that influences people's overall well-being.

When to Refer

At what point do you determine that someone needs a referral to an outside mental health resource? The simple answer is that when a person's needs are greater than what your church can provide, you should immediately move into the referral process. When you aren't sure what to do next and you need help, go ahead and refer. That's okay. The more nuanced answer is that depending on the resources in your church, that threshold may be crossed at a different point.

Let's talk first about the nonnegotiables. For any church that does not have a licensed mental health practitioner on staff providing confidential counseling services to parishioners, some symptoms or experiences are indicators that an immediate referral is needed. We will pay more attention to these crisis situations in chapter 4, but here's a quick list:

Suicidal or homicidal ideation. At the moment a congregant mentions they are thinking about hurting or killing themselves or someone else, a referral is required. It doesn't matter whether you think they are serious or not. It doesn't matter if you feel it is a "cry for help" or some form of manipulation. Seek emergency help, and don't delay.

Unusual sensory experiences or beliefs. If a congregant says they are hearing voices or seeing things, or has persistent beliefs that outside forces are controlling their thoughts, trying to harm them, or are out to get them in some way, you should act quickly. These could be signs of a psychotic or delusional disorder, and the person will likely need some form of medication for relief of these symptoms.

Serious substance abuse. If a member reports that they are using alcohol or prescription drugs in excess, or using illegal drugs, to the extent that they are unable to manage mood and stress, be available for family, or complete work tasks, they need immediate treatment that is outside the scope of what you can do.

Domestic violence or abuse of any kind. Whether the stated victim or the alleged abuser comes to you for support, domestic and interpersonal violence is outside of the scope of what should be handled in a church because of the possible legal implications for those involved and the risk of bodily harm to one or both of the people in the relationship. Christian values about marriage often cloud our view of the appropriate things to say to people involved in a domestic violence situation. It is best not to be the only source of support during these sensitive situations. If a child, elder, or person with disabilities is being abused or neglected, you should refer, and you also have a responsibility, to report to the appropriate social service agency.

Symptoms that prevent a person's ability to perform daily tasks. If a member reports that they are having significant trouble eating, sleeping, working, providing for their home or family, or anything of the sort, they need a level of care that typically cannot be provided in a church context. For all these reasons, it is best to refer to an outpatient mental health provider or agency for evaluation and treatment.

The instances listed above are grounds for an immediate referral to an outside provider. Other reasons might be more nuanced. In many churches various leaders have pastoral care roles: these can include hospital visitation, brief conversations and prayer with members, providing Scripture, and things of the sort. An additional layer of this process may be what is known as pastoral counseling. These are more formal meetings, most often held by pastors or ministers in the church, where a member sets an appointment to receive guidance and advice on a particular issue. In my master's thesis research, I asked pastors about their pastoral care activities, and a couple of things rose to the surface.[2] First, pastors engage in quite a bit of pastoral counseling—official meetings with parishioners focused on addressing particular issues—some as many as 50 percent of their pastoral time. Second, pastors counsel members on a variety of issues: family and marital concerns, job concerns, life changes, emotional problems, and more. While ministers can certainly provide some support and guidance, they cannot possibly provide expert advice on that wide a range of concerns. They aren't trained to do that! Third, pastors have a variety of responsibilities that they have to manage on a daily basis; as those demands mount, they are less able to provide parishioners with the level of care and support they need and deserve. They aren't lacking in desire, just in resources.

Because of the realities of pastoral care and counseling in the traditional church setting, there must be some limitations on what pastors and church leaders can provide. So, in addition to the clear-cut boundaries discussed above, I will here provide some other rules of thumb for knowing when to refer to an outside resource. If, after meeting with a member a few times, it seems that they are showing very little improvement or their symptoms have worsened, you should refer. If there is an actual mental health diagnosis at play, you don't want to delay the person's access to treatment and prolong their recovery process. If the person seems to be asking for more and more of your time, is having difficulty respecting personal boundaries, or seems to be more and more dependent on you and your guidance, it's time to refer. While we want the church to function as a source of support, we don't want it to become a crutch so that people do not feel capable of managing their own lives. Finally, if you have the sense that your help is inadequate, that the person's problems are outside the scope of what you are able to help with, it's time to refer.

The following is a list of symptoms that serve as signs that professional help is needed:

- repeated, frequent crying spells
- increasing substance use
- feelings of being hopeless, helpless, or worthless
- worry or panic that interferes with work or leisure activities
- emotional instability or irrational behavior
- consistent problems with short-term memory, concentration, or decision making
- engagement in risky or unusual behaviors (overspending, unsafe sex practices, drastically reduced need for sleep, self-injury)
- social withdrawal or isolation

Referring a member to a resource outside the church *does not mean that the church no longer serves as the well*. It just means that the way the well functions adjusts some. A referral to someone outside the church is not an indication that we don't believe in the power of God to heal and deliver. In fact, it is our affirmation that God works through people, systems, and even medications to provide healing. This referral is not an implicit message that the member is unlovable, unsavable, or unwelcome at the well. In fact, we need to work explicitly to make sure the opposite message comes across loudly and clearly: *We love you so much that we will do whatever we can to help you to find wholeness. We love you too much to let our own shortcomings negatively impact your healing!*

43

Readiness at the Well

Let's return again to John 4. Jesus and the Samaritan woman were engaged in a debate of sorts. He understood her inadequacies and decided to be in conversation with her anyway. She reminded him of why he shouldn't be talking to her, and he was undeterred. Jesus said to her "If you knew the gift of God, and who it is that is saying to you, 'Give me a drink,' you would have asked him, and he would have given you living water." I can imagine the incredulous look on the woman's face as she replied, "Sir, you have no bucket, and the well is deep" (vv. 10-11). How could he possibly give her water? Only a few minutes earlier he was asking her for a drink. And now he claimed to be able to give her water when he had nothing with which to draw it! How could this be?

She was talking about literal water, and Jesus was trying to shift her attention to a spiritual conversation about God and salvation. In verses 13-14 he said, "Everyone who drinks of this water will be thirsty again, but those who drink of the water that I will give them will never be thirsty. The water that I will give will become in them a spring of water gushing up to eternal life." Some might look at this passage and see it as a call to focus on the spiritual over the natural—many churches take this stance. But Jesus was inviting her to expand her scope, to see different ways for her problems to be solved, to be seen and understood in a way that hadn't been possible before. This is what we offer when we have the skills and structures in place to address people's needs. It's an invitation to bring everything—natural and spiritual—into the community for sharing and healing.

Too often people use the church as a filling station. When we are spiritually or emotionally depleted, we go to get our tanks filled. This process works, in that if we keep going regularly, we don't have to stay in an empty place for very long. However, this gas-tank Christianity requires that we actually come to the church to be filled. If we can get there, great! If we can't, then what? Jesus' admonition to the Samaritan woman can be useful to all of us. God has the capacity to serve *more* than our immediate spiritual needs. When the church is at its best, we don't have to operate from a deficit model. We can have relationship with God and one another that becomes a renewable resource! When people can bring *all* their needs to the church—not just the spiritual ones—the totality of life becomes more sustainable and life-giving. True ministry for mental health affirms God's ability to work wonders in every facet of our lives. It is our living out of Luke 1:37: "Nothing will be impossible with God."

Culture Questions

■ How often do people in your church seek out ministers and other leaders for emotional support and guidance?

■ Do you have any leaders or parishioners with mental health training or experience who can help direct you to appropriate community resources?

■ What is your assessment of the kinds of issues your parishioners tend to need help with?

■ What ongoing processes do you have in place to assess mental and emotional health in your church body?

■ What are the ways in which your church leaders and members talk publicly about mental illness and mental health?

Well Points

■ When we manage stigma and build relationships, people will be more open with talking about mental health concerns.

■ Plan ahead! Get ready to deal with mental health concerns before they actually happen.

■ Conversational readiness includes listening and reflecting, which allow us to see and understand people at a deep level.

■ Structural readiness involves building a "master list" of resources that is easily accessible to the whole church.

■ Transference of trust is a process by which we refer people to a professional provider while assuring them that we believe that the referral will be helpful.

Notes

1. Forum for Theological Exploration, "The FTE Guide to VocationCARE," 2012, https://fteleaders.org/uploads/files/GUIDE%20TO%20VOCATIONCARE%202012%20Low.pdf

2. Jessica Young Brown, "More Than a Prayer: Pastors' Perceptions of Mental Health Services," (2010).

CHAPTER 4

Cautions and Crises

In this chapter we discuss and plan for the rare but real possibility that someone in your congregation might experience a mental health crisis. I say this is rare because media coverage and popular discussions about mental health symptoms lead people to believe that everyone with mental health concerns is in a mental health crisis! The pervasive stigma in the popular media related to mental health steers people to think of mental illness and danger as synonyms. The reality, however, is that the "boring" stories do not make the news. As we discussed earlier, about one in five American adults is likely to have a diagnosable mental health condition. However, when we think about serious mental illness, a mental health condition that severely impacts a person's ability to work, build healthy relationships, or adapt to the environment, that number drops to about one in twenty-five people.[1] Folks with serious mental illness are the people at greatest risk for some kind of mental health crisis that might require immediate medical attention. So we will take a moment to focus on how we can best serve them. We will also tackle ways we can address the crisis situations most likely to occur: suicide and suicidal ideation, risk of harm to others (including domestic violence), psychotic symptoms, and dangerous substance abuse.

In Genesis 41 we find Joseph, once abandoned and sold by his brothers into slavery, now in a position of high esteem in Egypt, advising the pharaoh. Having become known for his great wisdom, Joseph was often consulted on important issues facing the kingdom. At this point in time, Joseph's adept interpretation of the pharaoh's dreams had revealed that while the nation of Egypt was currently in a season of plenty, soon would come seven years of devastating famine. Joseph's wise counsel to the pharaoh was this:

> Now therefore let Pharaoh select a man who is discerning and wise, and set him over the land of Egypt. Let Pharaoh proceed to appoint overseers over the land, and take one-fifth of the produce of the land of Egypt during the seven plenteous years. Let them gather all the food of these good years that are coming, and lay up grain under the authority of Pharaoh for food in the cities, and let them keep it. That food shall be a reserve for the land against the seven years of famine that are to befall the land of Egypt, so that the land may not perish through the famine.' (vv. 33-36)

In other words, if the people of Egypt were to survive the impending turmoil, it was essential that they prepare. This preparation must be comprehensive, strategic, and forward-facing. Had they waited until the famine actually occurred, the whole kingdom would be in danger of starvation. They could see no current signs of famine. In fact, things were going great! Everyone was eating well; farmers were prosperous and the kingdom was flourishing. Still, they were now aware that things could change suddenly. This is the way we must think about ministry for mental health. The strategies presented in this book will help us to work toward a church that is poised to have healthier relationships and greater mental wellness. Still, we must prepare for the worst.

Before we get into the specifics of these situations, it's important to set some basic guidelines for handling these types of crises in general. The first guideline is one we discussed in chapter 3: be prepared! A high-stress situation is not the time when you want to have to do the legwork of making crucial life-and-death decisions. So establish a solid process for managing crises before one occurs.

Identify the resources in your area for the myriad challenges you might face. It is better to err on the side of caution and have what you consider to be too many resources than to be in a situation where you need information and don't have it at your disposal. In addition to mental health or substance abuse concerns, when a child or vulnerable adult is in a situation where they are experiencing abuse or neglect, church leaders are mandated by law to report to the social service agency that manages these cases. Local agencies often have hotlines a person can call to ask whether a situation is reportable.

You might consider developing a list of suicide hotlines, local mental health agency crisis numbers, domestic violence hotlines, and substance abuse resources, such as recovery houses and locations for Alcoholics Anonymous and Narcotics Anonymous meetings. Suicide hotlines or warm lines are twenty-four-hour resources where someone who is feeling suicidal can reach out for a person to talk to. These are best suited for people who are suicidal and in distress but do not have a plan or intent to harm themselves. Domestic violence hotlines connect victims with housing resources, strategies for leaving an abusive situation, and connecting with domestic violence counselors. Substance abuse resources help people dealing with addiction to get connected to detox or other services as quickly as possible. Alcoholics Anonymous and Narcotics Anonymous are places of accountability and support for people working to stay free from substance abuse.

Of course, when you have doubt about what resource is most appropriate in an emergency, you can always call 911; dispatchers are trained to connect you with the right emergency responders. If the situation is urgent but not life-threatening, call the local government-run mental health agency, and crisis responders can connect you with resources for the particular concern. Posting or having this list of resources readily accessible when a crisis arises is vital. One person should not be the "holder" of this information.

Instead, it should be accessible to a wide variety of people so that no one has to jump through multiple hoops to obtain it. Consider having a room set aside at your church for having sensitive conversations to protect people's confidentiality, and post the list there.

Signs of a Mental Health Crisis

Next, let's discuss some general signs or symptoms that might suggest that a crisis is occurring. In chapter 3 we talked in general about when a referral to a mental health professional might be warranted. The best-case scenario is that someone comes to a leader and discloses that something is wrong, such as domestic violence or substance abuse. When this happens, it is easy to identify that some emergency action needs to be taken so the person is supported. However, in some situations, people are unable to recognize and communicate their own needs, so they need our help.

Let's return to the conversation about relationships in chapter 2. The benefit of persisting in relationships, of pursuing people when they push us away, is that we get to know them. We begin to understand their behavioral patterns, their personalities, and their way of being in the world. This knowledge is vitally important, because when we have this information, we can recognize and respond to any drastic behavioral or personality changes. This is one of the first signs they may be in crisis. Let's say, for example, that you have a parishioner who is usually happy and outgoing, and you notice that for the past few Sundays they seem withdrawn and sad. Or perhaps a person who is usually dependable and conscientious ends up missing several responsibilities and someone else must pick up their dropped balls. Rather than writing off this out-of-character behavior as some kind of personal failing, consider that it might actually be a cry for help. Remember, *bad behavior is the result of an unmet need*. At this point, you don't know what is causing the unusual behaviors, but you can make a guess that something is wrong. So your next response is to ask the person a question. As we've already discussed, language matters, so you need to figure out a way to communicate your concern and acknowledge behaviors that might be a problem without shaming or condemning the people you want to be in relationship with. Keep in mind that your goal is to help them, not run them off. Here are some suggestions:

> "Sister Jones, I noticed that you missed a few meetings in a row, and you're usually such a regular attender. Has something been going on? How can I help?"
>
> "Brother Smith, a couple of members mentioned to me that you pushed past them on Sunday as you were leaving church, to the point that one person almost fell. This doesn't seem like your usual style. Did something happen to make you upset?"

Notice the formula used in both of these examples. First, the specific observed behavior is named. Second, the unusualness of the behavior is mentioned. Third, an offer of help or support is made. Also note that in neither of the above examples is there an intimation that the person has angered, upset, or frustrated another. Not that it hasn't happened! This just isn't the time to share that information.

Now, let's return to our hypothetical conversation. Suppose Sister Jones lets you know that she has been feeling down and depressed. At that point, you could provide referrals for a couple of therapists whom you've already vetted. But what happens if she says that not only has she been depressed, but she has been drinking more, sleeping less, and even considering suicide? Here's where your previously prepared crisis plan comes into play.

The same red flag issues I briefly introduced in chapter 3 may demand crisis intervention in the short-term. Here we will return to each of those red flags and expand on what processes you as a church should have ready in the event they occur.

Suicidal Ideation

One of more common issues you may encounter when you invite people to be honest about their emotional experiences is *suicidal ideation*. At the moment a congregant mentions they are thinking about hurting or killing themselves, a referral is required. It doesn't matter whether you think they are serious or not. It doesn't matter if you feel it is a "cry for help" or some form of manipulation. Still (and I'm sure you know this by now!) you are not going to throw a business card at them and walk away. What you need to determine is whether their situation warrants an immediate call to 911, or if they simply need a swift referral to a provider.

For many of us, suicide is a very scary thing to talk about. We don't like to think about death, and we certainly don't want to consider that it could be at our own hands. Many black folks believe African Americans do not commit suicide—that we are too strong, too faithful, too invincible to succumb to something as "weak" as suicide. However, both the research and my own personal clinical experience suggest quite the opposite. While suicide rates for African Americans are lower than for white people and Native Americans, about 6 out of 100,000 black Americans commit suicide each year. In addition, an alarming pattern is emerging among black adolescents. They are more likely than any other demographic group to have attempted suicide in the last year, and are more likely than other groups to need medical intervention due to the severity of these attempts. In a 2017 study of risk behaviors, nearly 10 percent of black high school students reported a suicide attempt in the last year.[2] *Ten percent.* One in ten. This is a frightening reality! We can no longer pretend that we are immune. Stigma is, quite literally, killing us.

Because suicide is such a dangerous reality, we cannot overestimate its seriousness. Most of us, however, have no experience with talking about it. Because of the way we sometimes see faith as incompatible with mental health struggles, some of us might even believe that suicide is evil or sinful in some ways. We might even be concerned that if we talk about it or acknowledge it, we may increase the likelihood of a person following through with such acts. This is just not true. Here I want to make a crucial point: most people who think about committing suicide *do not actually want to die.* For the vast majority of people who experience suicidal ideation, this process is a response to an intense feeling of hopelessness and despair, and it feels like the only possible way to get any relief from the unbearable pain they are feeling at the moment. A major gift we can give to people is to provide a sense of hope and to present an option for escaping the pain.

A simple research-based process for asking the important questions about suicide is called Question, Persuade, Refer (QPR).[3] Though there is extensive literature and training on how to execute this model, which I encourage you to seek out, I will provide the basics here:

■ Step 1: question. *Ask directly if a person has been thinking about or planning for suicide.* Sometimes a person will tell you directly that they have been thinking about taking their life. Other times they may give indirect "hints," such as "I just don't see any point in the future" or "There's no point in any of this." You should respond with immediacy to either kind of response. Example: "Are you saying that you have been thinking about taking your own life?" If the answer in any way approximates a yes, the next step is to call 911 or a crisis intervention line immediately and remain with the person until a mental health professional can evaluate their safety and provide you with some next steps for how to care for the person.

■ Step 2: persuade. *Persuade the person to seek out professional help.* Lots of variables might influence how well this conversation will go, which I won't elaborate on here. In short, you want to provide the person with an alternative to suicide—getting help and not feeling the way they feel now. This could be something such as, "I know that sometimes life can be overwhelming. But there are people who can help you to feel better so things are more manageable. Can we make a call to a crisis line or a therapist who can work with you?" You might also make a personal connection here: "You know, I've been to a counselor, and they really helped me to figure out ways to manage my stress." Perhaps you remind the person that the church is already prepared for situations like this. "Did you know that the church has a list of counselors to help with issues just like this? Let's give one a call." The best-case scenario is that the person agrees to seek out help, which moves you to the third step.

■ Step 3: refer. *Get the person connected with a professional who can provide mental health support.* Because of your commitment to relationship and your deep awareness of the severity of the situation, if someone even hints at suicide, it is your responsibility to get them connected with a professional in a tangible way. This means making the phone call with them or even escorting them to the emergency room or driving/accompanying them to a first appointment. If a person expresses a plan or an intent to act on that plan, they should be taken to an emergency room right away, and someone should stay with them while the assessment process is initiated. This is pastoral care at work. You become the hands and feet of Jesus. No sheep is abandoned. If the person denies wanting to die or desiring to kill themselves, you can slow down this process a bit, but a referral should still be made within a week or so, and you should move into an active pastoral care role.

In addition to having the list of providers readily available, preparation for an encounter with suicidal ideation might include having a training for the congregation on a structure like QPR or

Mental Health First Aid.[4] These programs are often provided free or at low cost to community organizations. They are especially crucial for church ministers and leaders but can be beneficial for the entire congregation.

Domestic Violence

The next issue for which you need some specialized preparation is *domestic violence*. Domestic violence (DV) is challenging to address because victims often choose to keep what is happening to them secret for fear of retribution from the perpetrator, shame, or judgment. They might minimize or even lie about what is going on at home. Because of our values surrounding marriage, this is often a particularly challenging issue for churches. We see marriage as a religious covenant that is permanent in nature. Spouses should "cleave" to each other and be prayerful about how to meet each other's needs.

I am aware that this discussion about domestic violence sets up marriage as heterosexual by default and that many families in our churches might not fit this model, but I do not want to do a disservice to the LGBTQIA community here by trying to squeeze in a hurried discussion of the complex issue of sexual orientation in the black church. In short, individuals who are same-gender loving experience increased social stigma and are at greater risk for emotional distress due to the possible judgment and even exile to which they might be exposed. I will share some more about this in chapter 6. For now we will focus on how churches respond to domestic and intimate partner violence in heterosexual relationships, particularly marriages.

While men can be the victims of domestic violence, the overwhelming majority of DV is perpetrated by men upon women. This is not because men are inherently bad or malicious, but it is a reflection of the power that men are given in a patriarchal society where men often have decision-making privilege and power over women. The church participates in this structure. Some churches relegate women to certain aspects of service or leadership. Many churches do not recognize the ability of women to lead in pastoral or other influential leadership roles. Many black churches are steeped in a traditional Christianity that reinforces dynamics in which the man is allowed, and even encouraged, to exert excess power over his wife and daughters. A classic example of this is an interpretation of the Ephesians 5 text we so often hear at Christian weddings that leads to valuing of the husband as the functional and spiritual head of the household, with the wife submitting to him.[5] Therefore, when a woman comes forth and admits there are unhealthy dynamics in a relationship, the inclination might be to encourage her to return home and work on things with her husband. A minister might suggest that she stop and pray, and that the couple seek the counsel of other couples. The minister may even remind her that marriage in the Christian context is a permanent covenant. All these things are great guidance in the context of a wide assortment of marital conflicts. However, domestic violence deserves special attention.

How do we distinguish between marital conflict and a potential domestic violence issue? In general, DV is any situation where one partner seeks to exert power or control over the other by using verbal, physical (including sexual), or emotional assaults.[6] An individual may talk about not being able to express themselves or engage in certain actions for fear of angering their partner. They might express being scared or uneasy at home. It is important to note that physical violence is not the only indicator of DV. Persons could report being forced into unwanted sexual encounters, being physically restrained, not having access to household money, or being relegated to certain areas of the house. In many cases, emotional and verbal violations happen earlier and more often. DV can also encompass one partner controlling all of the money or lines of communication in a family. It can involve verbal insults, emotional attacks, name-calling, and humiliation. These relationship dynamics are reinforced by and lead to poor mental health outcomes for *both* partners, and they result in a dangerous emotional environment that can escalate over time. The most important thing church leaders can do in the face of a possible DV situation is ensure that the person doing the reporting is safe. Rather than starting with religious messages on the permanence of marriage, our first responsibility is to make sure people have the resources they need. Ask the person directly if they feel safe to return home. Have a list of counselors who focus on domestic violence, as well as a list of shelters or other resources readily available. Have the person identify and connect with all their sources of support—family, friends, and others. If both partners are a part of the church, it is also necessary to reach out to the alleged perpetrator, as they may be in need of support. However, it is only appropriate to do this after you are sure the victim is safe from retribution (staying with someone, staying in a shelter, etc.). It is also appropriate, and necessary, to encourage partners to be prayerful about their marriage. But the key here is that we *should not* blindly encourage people to stay in unsafe relationships. These dynamics require a more nuanced approach. When these situations involve children, or adults who are incapacitated in some way, they require a report to the proper social service agency. In most states, clergy are mandated reporters for child abuse and neglect, as well as elder abuse. Reporting laws may be state-specific, so you should check your state to determine the specific requirements. RAINN, a national organization focused on educating about abuse and sexual violence, provides a quick tool to research your state laws.[7]

Unusual Sensory Experiences

The next symptom of serious mental illness is *unusual sensory experiences or beliefs*. The most common psychotic symptom that might occur among church people is hearing voices. Many people with this affliction describe hearing one or more voices and have the sensation that they are overhearing conversations or hearing people mumbling. This symptom is more dangerous if people say the voices are talking directly to them, telling them to do things, such as hurt themselves or others (called "command voices"). Either way, this is an immediate sign to contact a professional mental health provider.

Other people might report seeing things that aren't there. A caveat here is that as Christians, we believe in things we cannot see. That is the foundation of our faith! We believe that God speaks to us, that we can see visions, and that the miraculous can occur. At the same time, we can acknowledge that some unusual or extrasensory experiences are outside our religious system and may mean people need additional support. As a general rule, if the vision, sound, or other sensation is outside of what can be explained by a religious experience in your context, and especially if the person is distressed, you should help them seek outside help immediately. Refraining from arguing with the person or trying to dissuade them from their beliefs is essential. If a person is truly having a psychotic episode, this process might only agitate them and make them less likely to reach out for support in the future.

If you have concerns about the person's ability to understand what is happening, make sure a family member or friend is aware of the situation and can attend an appointment with them. If the person has no family member or friend for support, someone in the church needs to step into that role. As usual, provide a referral, and then remain a support as a pastoral care provider—pray, check in, and work to help the person connect with their faith as a part of your community. It is also a good idea for someone to provide information to the professional about what has been observed, in case the person is unable to share all of their symptoms. While mental health professionals are bound by law and ethics to keep whatever they discuss with a client confidential, they can accept collateral information that is reported to them.

Substance Abuse

The final issue that may require crisis intervention is *substance abuse*. Signs that alcohol use may be out of control include a person feeling that they cannot go more than a few days without using alcohol, spending money allocated for bills on drinks, or being frequently intoxicated or hungover. If a person reports using illegal substances, especially in excess, they may need intervention. Anytime substance use is disrupting work, causing conflict in the family, or resulting in changed behavior, it is probably time to intervene. Another growing concern is the misuse of prescription drugs. People struggling with this issue may engage in "doctor shopping" to get new medications, "borrow" medications from family members and friends, or become dependent on taking pills to be productive at work and home. People with more severe substance use disorders might steal from family members to pay for substances and spend excessive time inebriated, recovering from being under the influence, or searching for the next high.

Because substance use disorders are notoriously hard to treat, this is another concern that requires the immediate intervention of a professional mental health provider. If a person shows up at church and you suspect they are under the influence, you have some decisions to make. From my perspective, if a person is not disruptive, it probably makes sense to let them be and have someone pull them aside after church to check in. If they are disruptive, it is better to escort them to a private room and give them a chance to sober up before having a discussion about next steps. Either way, follow the template: name the behavior, express your concern about it, and provide a resource.

Preparation Is Key

The take-home message about preparedness for all of these issues is a simple one. First, have resources available before the crisis occurs. Gather a group of people in a room and have them consider all the issues that could occur in your church, then come up with a list of desired resources. Consult mental health professionals and social service agencies about the resources available in your area. Have leaders role-play having challenging conversations with parishioners so that they feel comfortable broaching difficult topics. Finally, don't avoid or wait to address the concerns listed above. Address them head-on! Crises require that we act quickly and decisively. The issues discussed above could involve life-or-death situations. Preparation is key!

As I close this chapter, I want to return your attention again to the well scene in John 4. Remember that our frame here is that the church is a well where people can receive what they need if we are who God is calling us to be. When we left Jesus and the Samaritan woman at the end of chapter 3, he was telling her about the possibility for spiritual water that would quench her thirst permanently! This piqued the woman's interest to the extent that she asked for the water so she no longer would have to come to the well and suffer the humiliation of her second-class status. She thought Jesus was giving her an out—a way to avoid the community with which she had not been able to engage. His response was to tell her to go call her husband, and she replied that she had none. This, of course, Jesus already knew. On a first reading, it may seem Jesus was trying to call attention to the things she had done in the past and shame her into feeling bad for them. But what I see here is Jesus wanting her to grasp that he knew and understood her at a deep level. Even what could be thought of as her greatest shame was not enough to turn his attention away from her or make her ineligible for his help.

Paradoxically, Jesus pointing out the woman's issue did not alienate her from the community. She had been experiencing disconnection for years, but naming what ailed her seems to have had the impact of reuniting her with those from whom she had been estranged. Her response was to run back to the city and connect with the very people she had been avoiding! "Come and see a man who told me everything I have ever done! He cannot be the Messiah, can he?" she cried (v. 29). It was *her* invitation that actually drew the attention of the whole community to Jesus. We will return to this point in chapter 5, but I want to point out that this reconnection of the Samaritan woman with the community could only have happened once Jesus made it very clear to her that he could handle all her "mess." He asked a question, which drew attention to behavior that would not allow her to be well. His attention to and naming of her symptoms was to send a message: *I see you, and I can help you. I won't be another person to abandon you or write you off.* Can you feel the power there? This is what we offer people when we are prepared for the worst. What feels like a crisis to them can be met with steadiness and security by us. This is the beauty of the well.

Culture Questions

■ What are the key mental health and social service resources in your area? How can you create an exhaustive list that is easily accessible to leaders and laypersons alike?

■ How comfortable are your leaders with discussing sensitive issues? What preparation or training do you need to be able to provide resources with confidence and calm?

■ How do your theological beliefs about mental illness, substance abuse, and marriage inform how you address related crisis situations? What can you do to help separate what you see as right and wrong from the immediate needs of ensuring wellness and safety?

■ What implicit and explicit messages about mental health, suicide, domestic violence, or substance use do you send through preaching, teaching, and programming?

Well Points

■ Some situations require immediate crisis intervention and a swift plan of action.

■ Identify resources ahead of time so you won't need to search for them during a crisis situation.

■ Building deep relationships allows us to see and respond to behaviors that might indicate that a crisis is happening.

■ When you see a behavior that warrants immediate response, use this formula: Name specific behavior + express concern + provide resources.

Notes

1. National Alliance on Mental Illness, "Mental Health by the Numbers," NAMI, accessed January 2, 2019, www.nami.org/learn-more/mental-health-by-the-numbers.

2. American Foundation for Suicide Prevention, "Suicide Statistics," AFSP, April 16, 2019, https://afsp.org/about-suicide/suicide-statistics/.

3. Paul Quinette, "Gatekeeper: Suicide Prevention Training," *PsycEXTRA Dataset*, January 2007, 1–38, https://doi.org/10.1037/e537222009-001.

4. Mental Health First Aid, "Find a Mental Health First Aid Course," October 18, 2013, www.mentalhealthfirstaid.org/take-a-course/find-a-course/.

5. "Wives, submit yourselves to your own husbands as you do to the Lord. For the husband is the head of the wife as Christ is the head of the church, his body, of which he is the Savior. Now as the church submits to Christ, so also wives should submit to their husbands in everything" (Ephesians 5:22-25, NIV).

6. Centers for Disease Control and Prevention, "Intimate Partner Violence: Prevention Strategies," accessed November 5, 2019, www.cdc.gov/violence prevention/intimatepartnerviolence/prevention.html.

7. "Laws in Your State," RAINN, www.rainn.org.

CHAPTER 5

Expression and Exhortation

A beloved tradition in the black church is what in my church was called "prayer and praise" service. In my home church, this was a period of communal, unstructured time where people could sing songs, pray, and testify about the goodness of God as they were led. Because we are a people who deeply value ritual, some of us may remember a familiar refrain: "First giving honor to God, who is the head of my life. . . ." This statement was a reminder of our shared covenant to commit to that which God is calling us, to remember at all times that our blessings and challenges are orchestrated by an almighty God, and to ground the comings and goings of our lives in our faith. This statement provides an anchor—a way of understanding our lives and making meaning of them. After this common introductory statement, the testimony usually includes some common elements: offering prayer and praise to God, a witness to what trials and tribulations may have been overcome in the distant and recent past, a revelation about a current struggle or concern, and a request that the other members in the church pray with and for the testifier. It is an invitation into communal intercession and watching for an answer from God: "Those who know the words of prayer, please call my name!"

Some researchers have tried to understand exactly what happens in the testimony experience. Why is it such a vital part of life in the black church? Ezra Griffith, John Young, and Dorothy Smith suggest that testimony serves two purposes.[1] On a personal level, testimony is an expression of a personal experience with Christ that is almost indescribable other than it being a deeply personal religious experience. On a different level, it is a communal experience that exhorts (encourages) the whole community into moments of praise, worship, and connection with the Holy Spirit. Cheryl Townsend Gilkes describes testimony or "prayer and praise" service as a therapeutic experience that can literally serve as a treatment for mental health concerns: "It is at once a communication to fellow members that they understand their troubles and a way of communication to the Lord that this brother or sister's trouble is like their own."[2] So then, testimony is not just a ritualistic act. It is a powerful way of understanding and encountering God in the safety of a faith community. Testimony is, in and of itself, a healing process that can change the perspective and experience of both the testifier and those bearing witness to God's goodness and movement in their lives.

Testimony services are often embedded with beloved traditions and rituals, from sayings to physical gestures, to spirited "Amens" spilling from those listening to the testimony. They are cues for the community that set the stage for the spirit and intention of our time together. They are expressions of our faith. While some forms of tradition conjure for many of us ("church babies") a sense of warmth and familiarity, other traditional sayings or clichés do not make us feel connected and grounded. Instead, they lead people to feel isolated and shamed. Take for instance the saying "If you're going to pray, don't worry. If you're going to worry, don't pray!" That sounds good until your anxiety is uncontrollable and you can't get it out of your head. It's not a long road before people start believing their worrying is an indication of their failing as a believer. In fact, we have basically told them that!

Here's another one: "I thank God that I'm clothed and in my right mind!" Well, what if someone *doesn't* feel they are in their right mind? What does it mean about them if God doesn't seem to have blessed them with the sound mind that everyone else is celebrating having in their possession?

A common misconception revealed in our typical language in the church is that people can change their thoughts and feelings through sheer force of will. I believe this is a misinterpretation of the many Scripture passages where people in the Bible are admonished to be courageous, to trust God, or to be confident. When we say these kinds of things without qualification to people who might be struggling with their mental or emotional health, we send an implicit message that they are somehow deficient as Christians when they cannot think or feel differently. This dynamic is a recipe to encourage pretending. It is an invitation to hide parts of yourself so you don't reveal yourself as unfaithful or unable to produce a shift in your situation. It is, essentially, an invitation *not* to testify. When people don't feel free to testify, we rob them of all the healing benefits testimony can provide.

As another example, many of us have heard sweeping assertions about how many times we find the statement "Fear not" in the Bible. The verdict is still out on exactly how many—certainly well over a hundred; however, our interpretation of these Scriptures is often literal: "Do not be afraid. Stop feeling that unacceptable feeling and learn to lean on God more." This, to me, sounds like an autocratic command. I would argue that because these statements are embedded in conversations between God and a person, they cannot be taken so literally. A quick sampling of some of these Scriptures suggests that a more nuanced interpretation might make more sense. Consider the following passages:

> Genesis 26:24: That very night the LORD appeared to him and said, "I am the God of your father Abraham: do not be afraid, for I am with you and will bless you and make your offspring numerous for my servant Abraham's sake."

> 1 Chronicles 28:20: David said further to his son Solomon, "Be strong and of good courage, and act. Do

not be afraid or dismayed; for the LORD God, my God, is with you. He will not fail you or forsake you, until all the work for the service of the house of the LORD is finished."

Luke 12:7: "Even the hairs of your head are all counted. Do not be afraid; you are of more value than many sparrows."

In the Genesis passage, Isaac was coming through a season of quarreling with all the different groups of people he had attempted to settle with, all while not being able to live in the land God had promised him many years earlier. He dealt with land disputes and jealousy from people who were experiencing a famine while he seemed to have much agricultural success. I can imagine that Isaac was tired, worn out, frustrated, and worried about when his family would find stability and peace. God reminded Isaac of the promise God made to Isaac's father to prosper and multiply their family.

In the verse from 1 Chronicles, David had just provided his son Solomon with the blueprint for the temple God had given him over a long period of time. Though David received the vision, it was Solomon's responsibility to bring it to fruition and to build it according to very specific instructions: quite a task! This passage is interesting because there is no clear indication in the text that Solomon protested or implied that he was fearful. David provided encouragement to his son because it was something that was needed at the time. He loved his son, and he knew Solomon had been assigned a daunting task, so David gave his son something he needed *before* Solomon even had the chance to realize that he needed it. As the church mothers would say, "Ain't God good?"

In the verse taken from the book of Luke, Jesus was warning his disciples to be on guard against Pharisees who meant them no good. He admonished them that they should be vigilant but not afraid. Essentially, he was saying that they needed only to be concerned about how God viewed them, and he affirmed that they were already valuable in God's eyes. "You are important. You matter. God cares intimately about you." Jesus was preparing them for the persecution and accusations he knew were coming. God had revealed to him that their path would not be a traditional one, and that the group would face much opposition. Despite it all, he wanted to remind them they were taken care of.

Of course these are just a sampling. But in each of these cases, it seems that the "Fear not" is not at all about suspending or eliminating fear. In fact, the main players in each of the examples above are in a situation where it is completely natural and human to be worried or fearful! So then, perhaps "Fear not" is not a command to deny your human nature and be a robot; perhaps it really means something like this: "I know you're afraid. But you don't have to be. I'll take care of you."

How could there be an encouragement to "fear not" without an acknowledgment that the fear is real and present in our lives? Does God not know us intimately enough to know that the world can be a scary and daunting place, and that sometimes we feel ill-equipped, inadequate, or even doomed to fail? What if, instead of being a demand to act with resolute stoicism, "Fear not" is instead a warm embrace from a parent to a child: "I know you're scared, baby. I'm here." This critical difference is so meaningful and transformational. For folks whose fear is overwhelming, uncontrollable, and inexplicable, the latter assurance is a balm and the former demand serves as a rebuke.

"Don't worry" and "Fear not" are just two examples of the need to critically evaluate our religious language. Just because we have always said something doesn't mean we should continue saying it without qualifying or explaining what we mean. Remember what I said about stigma, that it is any negative attitude or belief that leads people to feel left out, less than, or unworthy in some way. Because the negative actions that result from stigma are so hurtful, often people who are dealing with mental health concerns are "on the offensive." As a method of protecting themselves, they might read between the lines. They might look for hidden meanings that confirm their fears that people find them unacceptable in some way. They might hear certain statements as rejection even if rejection is not our intention. To maintain acceptance in the community, they might decline to tell us what is really going on. They might feel ineligible to engage fully in the healing process of testimony. As the church, our responsibility is to evaluate both the intent *and* the impact of our words. There is a cost when we throw around terms like *bipolar* and *crazy* and *schizophrenic* as though they are adjectives for general use. There is a cost when we cavalierly dismiss strong emotional experiences such as fear or anxiety as disconnection from God or faith. People feel shut down, unheard, and alone. They don't have access to the exhortation that is such a vital part of the faith community. *Words matter.* We do ourselves a disservice if we pretend otherwise.

The Bible holds several examples of people being completely honest with God about their suffering, and God responding with care, not chastisement. The prophet Elijah, after conflict with King Ahab, ran into a cave and prayed to die: "I have had enough, LORD," he said. "Take my life; I am no better than my ancestors" (1 Kings 19:4, NIV). The Lord responded by sending an angel with bread and water. Only after Elijah had *forty days of rest and restoration* in the cave did the Lord return and encourage the prophet to get up and move. In psalm after psalm, David cried out to God about feeling forsaken and left behind. Take, for example, this passage from Psalm 34: "The righteous cry out, and the LORD hears them; he delivers them from all their troubles. The LORD is close to the brokenhearted and saves those who are crushed in spirit" (vv. 17-18).

Even Jesus, whom we could argue with certainty was totally connected spiritually and had the ultimate faith, was honest about his struggles. Two examples come to mind. First, in the garden of Gethsemane, Jesus admitted that he really did not want to die on the cross. He knew it was his purpose for being born in human form, and yet he felt open enough in his relationship with God to ask if there was any other way. "Father, if you are willing, remove this cup from me; yet, not my will but yours be done" (Luke 22:42). Note that this statement was not a communication that Jesus would disobey God or be rebellious in any way. It was an honest statement from a dedicated Son to a loving Father. Even as Jesus died on the cross, one of his last sayings was a desperate plea that seemed inconsistent with his knowledge that his death would not be permanent. In that moment, as Jesus sacrificed his own life for the lives of fallible humans like us, he took on and embodied one of the most challenging parts of humanness: we get scared, we can be unsure, and sometimes, though we know the very character of God, we become desperately afraid that we are all alone: "My God, my God, why have you forsaken me?" (Matthew 27:46).

Were these giants in our religious tradition experiencing failures of faith, or were they just expressing their humanness? An invitation into relationship with God is an invitation to bring the messy, doubtful, "crazy" parts of us and present them to God as an offering, as a request to be made whole. Wholeness is not even that these "bad" parts of us go away; it is simply our acknowledgment that God knows and accepts those parts of us along with the parts that are virtuous and bring us pride. When we are able to speak our deepest fears, God is able to respond directly to us in our point of need.

When we acknowledge that *all* of us struggle, that *all* of us wonder about where God is in our lives, and that *all* of us sometimes have doubts, we can include those who feel most alienated in our communities. One of my strategies whenever I am doing a workshop or presentation at a church is to somehow mention that I have a therapist. This is not because I want people to know my business. In fact, I am a very private person. But I share this part of my life because I want to normalize the process of needing support for mental health and wellness whenever I get an opportunity. Mental health is not just a medical intervention for people who are "crazy." Attending to mental health is something all of us need to do because we are human. What we know is that, in the black church, leaders set the stage. So a helpful strategy is for leaders to be honest about when they're struggling, how they get help, and the fact that mental health is an ongoing process, not a destination.

When we choose our language carefully, we send the overt message that our community is a place where everyone can get what they need. Perhaps in your church it means using "we" language instead of "they" language when talking about emotional struggles and mental health. Perhaps it means carefully considering our use of the word *crazy* or other derogatory terms that betray stigmatized attitudes. Perhaps it means we are careful about listening to people's concerns before we give them advice. Perhaps, rather than telling people what to do, we take a minute to acknowledge and empathize with how they feel and convey that God is equally as concerned with their suffering as God is invested in their deliverance. Expression matters. The words we choose have a real impact in the community of faith. This is only a restatement of a biblical truth: "Death and life are in the power of the tongue" (Proverbs 18:21). Choose your words carefully—choose life!

The beauty of choosing our language carefully is that we make the community of faith more accessible to those who desperately need to connect. It means we open up the testimony service and the possibility for receiving exhortation not just to those who have been delivered from "acceptable" things, but also to those who struggle with things that have previously been unspoken and unwelcome. Testimony service isn't just a ritualized act. Testimony service is a communal witness to that which God has done in the lives of others, so that we can gain strength for our own personal journeys. Testimony service allows us to mourn with those who weep and to rejoice with those who have found deliverance. Testimony service allows us to see that because God has moved in the life of someone we are in community with, God can also move in our personal situation. Testimony service is an impetus for community celebration! Imagine what can happen if, in addition to thanking God for being "clothed and in our right minds," we can also thank God for a therapist who helped us navigate a hard time, for a person who contemplated suicide but instead sought out help, or for a member who was beaten down by the burden of overwhelming depression but now has found relief through the right medications.

The great gift of testimony is that it encourages all of us to keep going. Testimony also has the capacity for evangelism. I'm not just speaking of evangelism in the context of saving souls, but of bringing the proverbial "lost sheep" back into the fold and renewing the faith of those who have become disconnected. Testimony can reconnect those who have previously found the church inadequate to address their life circumstances. Testimony makes space for *all* of our stories to be told and for everyone to be welcome at the well. When we make space for true ministry for mental health in the church, testimony service expands beyond physical healing, financial dispensations, and earthly possessions. Testimony can become about how a person has been delivered from the depths of depression, protected and covered in the midst of an abusive relationship, or ripped from the grasp of an overwhelming addiction. Furthermore, we serve a God who is big enough to deliver us in a multitude of ways: through prayer, therapy, medication, social support, and more! When we free people to tell their whole stories, we free the congregation to experience all of God's power!

Testimony at the Well

Let us return yet again to Jesus and the Samaritan woman at the well in John 4. When we left them, Jesus and the woman had just had an encounter that left her shocked and surprised. For her, Jesus' revelation of the details of her life confirmed that Jesus was a prophet. At the same time, though, she acknowledged there were still very real cultural differences between them. Her ancestors believed God was to be worshiped "on the mountain," while Jesus and his followers seemed to be saying that God should be worshiped "in Jerusalem." Jesus, however, was ultimately unconcerned with the things that separated them, sure that his coming, death, and resurrection had the capacity to unite everyone. He said, "The hour is coming, and is now here, when the true worshipers will worship the Father in spirit and truth, for the Father seeks such as these to worship him. God is spirit, and those who worship him must worship in spirit and truth" (vv. 23-24). In other words, let's not get caught up in things that, ultimately, are inconsequential. It doesn't matter where we worship. It doesn't matter what songs we sing or what our church building looks like. Our personal differences and idiosyncrasies should not separate us. All that matters is God and the gospel. If we focus on those essentials, we can deal with everything else.

At this, the woman's response was to leave her water jar, run back to town, and tell everyone what she had witnessed. She shouted that Jesus had told her everything about herself, and he must be the Messiah! The townspeople were so intrigued by what she said that they followed her to the well and came to meet Jesus for themselves. Later in the chapter we learn that "many Samaritans from that city believed in him because of the woman's testimony" (v. 39). Because of her testimony, they came to know Jesus for themselves. At the beginning of this story, the Samaritan woman was an outcast. She couldn't even come to the well in the morning like everyone else did because she had such intense shame about her life and her experiences. She was one who challenged Jesus; she had questions and concerns that she demanded he address before she could fully engage with what he was offering. But somehow, over the course of this encounter with Jesus, the outcast was transformed into an apostle. The woman who previously had no place at the well was now the one who gathered the community at the place of healing. It was her honest expression of her experience that caused the community to draw near to Jesus and accept the gospel.

Acknowledging here that the people in this town *knew* this woman is key. They had been complicit in her isolation and disconnection from the community because they all knew her story. But I imagine that before this very moment with Jesus, their role in her isolation had not been spoken about aloud, and certainly not in a way that would facilitate healing rather than ostracizing. They had witnessed the many men she had lived with. They had probably whispered about her during their morning trips to the well. (Let's be honest: that is what church folks sometimes do. We don't always live up to the aspirations of healthy community. Sometimes the people who need the most help are the ones we don't treat kindly. Their problems and struggles, especially if they dare to express them openly, challenge our desire to present ourselves as "faultless" and striving toward perfection.) The villagers probably looked down on her, judged her, and maybe even sent implicit and explicit messages that she was not welcome. Still, in the midst of all this, they could not ignore or dismiss what she was saying. Her testimony was so powerful and so captivating that they had to go see Jesus for themselves. Her testimony was so transformational, it removed the barriers that had probably existed for years between her and the community. Expression leads to exhortation. Telling the truth allows the whole community to be encouraged.

This is a process that can be replicated in all of our communities when we make space at the well for everyone. We can make space at the well when we work to ensure our language matches our values and conveys our desire to have everyone intimately connected to the community of faith. We can make space at the well when we stop trying to force people out of their moments of struggle and instead give them the opportunity to tell their stories. We make space at the well when every testimony is encouraged and valued. The people we may have counted out or given up on often have the most meaningful and compelling stories about what God can do. When the "lost" ones have an opportunity to share, we understand God in a deeper way. We are called to a higher level of faith and service. We connect with God and with others in ways that we never could have imagined. Testimony is powerful! Testimony transforms!

Culture Questions

■ What does your language convey about your true beliefs about mental health issues? How might your casual clichés impact people in ways you don't realize?

■ Are there people in your community who don't feel comfortable sharing their whole stories? What might be getting in the way of them fully connecting?

■ What are some ways you can begin to incorporate more inclusive language that recognizes the diversity of experience in your community?

■ Who in your leadership (or in your congregation) can take the lead as you make your community open for all stories to be heard?

Well Points

■ Testimony is an opportunity of connecting to the community.

■ Language impacts the ways people are able to engage with the church.

■ Mental health issues cannot be prayed or willed away.

■ The Bible provides examples of people sharing their struggles with God, and God responding with care and concern.

■ Adjusting our language opens up the ability of the whole community to engage in testimony and receive deliverance.

Notes

1. Ezra E. H. Griffith, John L. Young, and Dorothy L. Smith, "An Analysis of the Therapeutic Elements in a Black Church Service," *Psychiatric Services* 35, no. 5 (1984): 464–69. https://doi.org/10.1176/ps.35.5.464.

2. Cheryl Townsend Gilkes, "The Black Church as a Therapeutic Community: Suggested Areas for Research into the Black Religious Experience," *Journal of the Interdenominational Theological Center* 8, no. 1 (1980): http://digitalcommons.auctr.edu/itcj/vol8/iss1/8, 34.

CHAPTER 6

Digging the Well and Drawing from It

The church's mission is to bring people to Christ. That's the Great Commission and the ultimate goal that leads us to gather in community. One of the ways we execute this mission is by attending to people's mental health. When we engage in steps to create space at the well, people will become so engaged and connected in a healthy community that they will be led straight to Jesus!

So far we've talked about *silencing the stigma*, which helps people to feel accepted and engaged in the faith community. When they can be in community, we must live out *presence and persistence* so people can see and experience our intentional love for them and our determination to stick with them no matter what. As relationships develop, we must be ready to make *application* and take *action*—to put processes in place to manage people's concerns and help them get their needs met. Along this journey, we must recognize there are moments where we have to use *caution in crises*. Though these instances may be challenging in the moment, they ultimately provide us an opportunity to affirm that our intention is to stay in relationship and to help people access what they need. When all of that is executed, the product is a church where people are honest, authentic, and fiercely loving. This environment is the perfect breeding ground for *expression and exhortation*. This testimony is life-giving and sets us free! When we make space at the well, Jesus is made accessible. A loving community where Jesus is central *is* the Well!

By now, I'm sure you feel about ready to write a sermon on John 4! But humor me and return once more to the passage that has been guiding our journey together. I want to backtrack just a bit. When we left Jesus and the Samaritan woman, she had run from the well to the town to tell everyone about her experience with Jesus. Meanwhile, Jesus and the disciples were engaged in a conversation. When they returned to find Jesus speaking with the Samaritan woman, John 4 says they were "astonished" (v. 27) that he was speaking with her, but no one said a word to him. After she took her exit, they engaged in a conversation and Jesus taught them.

> Look around you, and see how the fields are ripe for harvesting. The reaper is already receiving wages and is gathering fruit for eternal life, so that sower and reaper may rejoice together. For here the saying holds true, "One sows and another reaps." I sent you to reap that for which you did not labor. Others have labored, and you have entered into their labor. (vv. 35-38)

For me, this verse returns to the mission of the church. We cannot lead people to Christ without first seeing and understanding them as human beings. The field *is* ripe for harvesting. We yearn for connection, support, and guidance. We crave relationship that will not hurt us or lead us to feelings of inadequacy. We have a deep desire to be seen and heard. Ministry that is attentive to the mental health of every parishioner is a means to the mission of bringing people to Christ! Throughout this book we have noted how Jesus attended to the needs of the Samaritan woman with complete disregard for social convention, her own conviction about her sense of inadequacy and disconnection in the community, and even her attempts to push him away. So then, the real message of this book is astoundingly simple: let's be like Christ!

Jesus was trying to get his disciples to understand that some of us do sowing and others of us do reaping. Creating space at the well is about understanding how small interactions over time can impact people at a personal and emotional level. These interactions may not always seem rewarding, and we won't always be clear on whether we've been successful. Caregivers know that trying to be in relationship with someone even when they push you away can be painful. And those on the care-receiving side face risks as well when they want to be honest with someone about their mental health struggles or have to work through fear about what their mental illness might really mean. Planning for crisis situations that we hope never happen is scary. Sometimes we won't even see the fruit of our labor. Because some of us sow and others of us reap, you may not see the impact of your kind interaction, encouraging word, or validating moment. But maybe a week or three months down the road, the person to whom you showed Christlike love will be ready to get the help they need. Maybe, because of the love and care they receive in your church, they will be able to connect with God at a deeper level and truly understand what it means to be in the safety of the Lord. Perhaps as your church culture grows and evolves, you will get a reputation for being a place where everyone can truly be themselves and where no one is cast out. I don't know about you, but just the thought of a church like that gives me goose bumps!

Digging the Well

My intention in the preceding chapters has been to give you a concrete framework for "digging the well" so that the faith community becomes a place where everyone has access to living water. Digging the well is really just preparation. It's about understanding that it takes time and energy to construct and maintain an environment where everyone can be healed. I do not presume that you have not already begun this process. I do not presume your current church environment is one that is hostile to people with emotional needs. I believe with everything in me that *all* of us are doing something right at this current moment. There is a reason people have remained connected to our churches all these years. The steps outlined in the preceding chapters are not an indictment of the past. They are a challenge for the future! As we examine and celebrate the things we are already doing to keep people in community, we can acknowledge that there is room for improvement. We are all doing something right, but no one is doing everything right. My hope is that we can celebrate even this, because imperfect churches can make great space for imperfect people. Based on the John 4 text that we have spent so much time in, we know that when the well is there and available, a relationship with Jesus will have transforming power! Our job is to set up the environment and let the Savior take it from there.

My prayer is that in reading this book you have found the material utterly accessible. As a mental health professional, I love consulting with churches and organizations about ways they can engage with members and with organizations in healthier ways to support the mental health of their members and the larger community. Many of my fellow mental health professionals also do this important, meaningful work. Still, the need is much greater than what we, individually or collectively, can accomplish. We live in a world full of people who have been tossed around by incredibly difficult life circumstances and victimized by those who were supposed to love them. Substance abuse, trauma, and pain are ubiquitous in our communities and in our churches. Some people might not ever make it to therapy or any form of professional counseling, but those people still need a place to "lay their burdens down." The church can be that place.

As I said in the introduction, the black church has always been a place where black folks could get resources for life. Historically, those resources have been spiritual, emotional, and even physical (there's nothing like a Baptist chicken dinner!). We also know that we live in a world that can be hostile and cruel to blackness, and that we have been forced to harden ourselves in response to a world that does not love and appreciate who we are or what we've been through. By accident, I believe, many of us have participated in our own dehumanizing by denying that we struggle, feel pain, and get tired. Generations of trauma have led to some ways of being that do not help us to be the healthiest versions of ourselves. The beautiful part is that our story does not end here. We have already within us the capacity to heal ourselves and our communities, and it all starts at the well!

What We Didn't Cover

For a variety of reasons, some issues have not been thoroughly addressed in this book. Perhaps those issues are the work for another book or another professional, but I want to at least mention one of them here so that it is on your radar. There are lots of ways people can be "othered" in the church, and these issues often intersect with mental and emotional concerns. One of those ways is one on which there is much scholarship, and it involves the large group of people who do not identify as heterosexual and may fall in one of the following categories: lesbian, gay, bisexual, asexual, or queer. In addition, there are people for whom the male/female genitalia of their birth do not feel like they match their internal experience; they identify as transgender or intersex. Together these folks are represented by the acronym LGBTQIA, and they are a vulnerable population in the world and in the church.

Many of our theological traditions and scriptural interpretations cause us to view LGBTQIA folks as sinful. While I do not share this belief, I won't get into a theological argument here; the bottom line is that regardless of what we believe about any person's identity as a "sinner," no one should be denied access to the well. LGBTQIA people are at greater risk for a variety of mental health concerns, including suicide, because they face discrimination and prejudice wherever they go. Add to this an identity as a black person, and membership in a faith system that is either ambivalent or actively hostile toward who they are, and you have a recipe for disaster! My prayer is that we as the black church can be a place where *all* are welcome and all have access to the well.

Historical Perspectives on Digging the Well

Much of the Old Testament describes people who were nomadic. When they moved from place to place, they took everything with them—tents, livestock, families—and started fresh in a new place. In ancient Israel there were two critical features at each settlement: an altar and a well. The altar was a physical expression of the importance of God as a central force in the functioning of the community. And the well was vital because it provided an essential human need—water.

Ronald Hyman provides a deeper, more contextualized understanding of everything the well meant for a community, beginning with the first mention of a well in the Bible in Genesis. In his discussion of the importance of wells for the physical survival of a community, Hyman says, "The successful digging of a well in those days required knowledge of the local terrain's potential to yield water, and the ability to protect it from envious neighbors who wanted to use the water or even take possession of the well itself. With success in digging and maintaining wells, people could obtain enough drinking water to sustain life."[1]

If we are to successfully dig the well, we must educate ourselves about our local terrain—about our church's culture. The Culture Questions at the end of each chapter were my attempt to help you understand the terrain at your particular church in your particular community. No two churches will have the exact same answers. Every congregation has different gifts and graces, so their way of addressing these issues will be most successful if they are reflective of the reality in which their church exists. We do ourselves a disservice when we compare what we are doing to the church down the street. Everyone will not dig the well the same way. For mental health ministry to be effective in your community, you will need to do some surveying. In each chapter, the suggested questions were prompts to get this surveying process going.

The process of assessing the needs in your area is an awesome opportunity to build a team of people whose passion can help your church do its absolute best to meet people's mental health needs. Hyman mentions that wells can also be a "locus for cooperation,"[2] noting that shepherds tending different flocks would often gather at the same well and might even wait until everyone had arrived so they could water their flocks at the same time. If a heavy stone covered the well, it might have taken more than one shepherd to move it so that everyone could access the well. While ministry for mental health at your church might not look like ministry for mental health at another church, the opportunities for collaboration are endless. Cooperation, not competition, is the key. In what ways might you link with another church or organization to share or maximize resources? What would it look like to have a community collaborative event such as a mental health fair or summit? Perhaps a church in the area has a private space for conducting pastoral counseling that could be used by multiple congregations. Space at the well is about removing every possible restriction you can think of so that everyone has access.

This point may seem in contrast to Hyman's assertion that part of the success of digging a well was "the ability to protect it from envious neighbors who wanted to use the water or even take possession of the well itself."[3] I would like to make two points here, one practical and one figurative. The figurative point here is that while we may face some competition, it's probably not actually for access to the well of the church. The fight is for the people whom we want to come to the well. Let's return to John 10:10, which we discussed in the introduction. The whole verse reads this way: "The thief comes only to steal and kill and destroy. I [Jesus] came that they may have life, and have it abundantly."

In Christendom, the first part of this verse is a common refrain. As black Christians in particular, we understand there are forces, some spiritual and some natural, that are working against our wholeness and health. Mental health stigma, and the complicated factors we have been discussing thus far, are forces the thief uses to steal, kill, and destroy. When we are so overcome by our worry about what people think about us that we don't reach out for help when we need it, our lives are stolen from us. When a lack of knowledge about mental health leads a family member to commit suicide, or to become so overwhelmed by addiction that they live a shell of a life, the enemy has killed someone we love. When our inability to understand and work through the trauma our family has experienced damages our relationships and causes them to be strained or estranged, our family has been destroyed. If we rest in the first part of the verse, we will become desolate and hopeless. We must remember, though, that we have the antidote!

If digging the well is our sustained attention to the realities faced by those we have been entrusted to care for and love on, then drawing from the well is a process by which we use that knowledge to guide people into the opportunity for abundant life. It means executing the skills we've been discussing and consistently evaluating and reevaluating the needs in our community so that people can be made whole. Drawing from the well is a continual process we never finish. It is a journey, not a destination. Just as the daily gathering of water was a necessity for life in biblical times, our commitment to love, support, and encourage one another on a daily basis is a necessity today.

Jesus' earthly ministry, though relatively short, revealed his commitment to understanding and relating to his followers as individuals.

Many of the miracles we love to discuss around the church deal with food. Jesus understood at a deep level that people could not take in a spiritual message if they had physical hunger. At other times Jesus allowed people to share their struggles, turmoil, and frustrations openly without chastising them. Let's look at one familiar example that shows how honest Jesus' relationships were. In John 11, Lazarus, a family friend, had been sick. By the time Jesus got to Bethany, Lazarus had died and his sisters were overwhelmed with grief. Martha, known for having a type-A personality, said, "Lord, if you had been here, my brother would not have died" (v. 21). She went on to say that she still believed, and Jesus did not chastise her for challenging him or for an open expression of grief. In fact, later in the chapter, we see that Jesus also wept at the death of Lazarus (see v. 35). Verse 35, "Jesus wept" (NIV), seems straightforward, but I've often had a question about it. In verse 23 Jesus responded to Martha's grieving, saying, "Your brother will rise again." Why then, later, when he *knew* he was about to raise Lazarus from the dead, would he weep?

Here's my take. First, Jesus was human. We celebrate his divinity and his perfection, but I think we lose sight of the fact that Jesus was a real person with real feelings who had real relationships and even real struggles. His good friend had died, and he, the Savior of the world, needed a moment to express his sadness at the loss, even though it was temporary. If Jesus had permission to cry, then surely we do too! Our salvation has never, ever required us to deny our humanness. That demand is and has always been a human construction. Second, I believe that Jesus, at his core, was relational. He lived in a way that suggests that he discerned, on a deep level, that connection must precede salvation. I can only imagine the relief Mary and Martha must have felt as he wept to know that they were not alone in their grief. I can also imagine that, having seen Jesus cry in that moment, they experienced Lazarus's eventual resurrection as that much more miraculous.

This is what space at the well looks like. Digging the well means we have a profound awareness that as the church, we must present a balm for people facing struggles "out there" in the world. To draw from the well, we must be like Jesus!

So now that you've read the book, what do you do next? My suggestion is that you start with the Culture Questions. Survey your church as a whole, then assemble a team of people for whom mental health is a passion and do an assessment of where your church is right now. Leadership should set priority areas and tackle those first. Maybe you can begin by working to eradicate stigma in your church. Start with a bulletin board or after-service program, and work your way from there. An effective way to use bulletin boards is by educating about awareness months like May, Mental Health Month; July, Minority Mental Health Month; and October, Domestic Violence Month. Once you've received some response to the Culture Questions, you have a starting point for what your particular church needs. Understand that when we talk about changing things like language or the small personal interactions we have with each other, change takes time! Leadership will need to model the behaviors your church is working toward, and there will be an adjustment period as people understand new ways of engaging with each other. Dedicating a few Bible studies or a sermon to going over these tips in greater detail would be helpful. In addition you may want to contact a mental health professional in your area and ask them to come in and do a consultation.

Closing Thoughts

I am fully aware that this book has not answered all your questions about mental illness, because I did not talk in detail about specific mental health conditions. That was intentional, because this book is really about serving everyone in the church regardless of whether they have a diagnosable condition. However, I have provided a brief primer in appendix B on common mental health conditions, which speaks to some of the particular presentations you might see in the African American community. I want to stress though that the diagnosis part is the work of professionals. The job of church leaders and laity is to care for people and love them. If there's one sentence that sums up all that you've read so far, it's this: *Our job is to make space at the well by being like Jesus.*

I've learned from years of clinical practice that often people's lived experience is not as clean-cut as the diagnostic manual would suggest. While diagnosis is helpful from a clinical perspective in that it informs what kind of treatment will be most effective, the most important thing to consider when addressing mental health issues is that people are having very human problems and are often suffering with connection. Life is messy! We can't always categorize it in neat little boxes, and we can't always make sense of it in ways that resolve all the questions we have. What we can do is move forward, knowing that God's intention for us is that we live abundantly and operate in wholeness.

I believe that most people have in them what they need to be well and whole. However, over the course of their lives, unhealthy circumstances, traumatic events, unbalanced relationships, and life in general may have led them to a point where they feel overwhelmed, confused, and frustrated. My job as a mental health professional is to help people find the resources they already have at their disposal to be healed. Our responsibility as the church is to support and undergird people as they journey toward healing and wholeness; to walk with them in their unfinished, sometimes devastated state; to make space at the well so they have access to the saving power of Jesus Christ.

In my clinical practice, I often use a simple analogy to remind clients that we are all, as humans, skilled at adapting to environments. This is a key feature of mental health and wellness. I encourage them to imagine that, in the family they grew up in, everyone played a particular game—maybe basketball or soccer or tennis. This game represents the communication patterns in a family, the way people express emotions, respond to stress, show love for each other, and set boundaries with one another. Whatever the game was, because kids are *experts* at adapting to the environment, the game that was played in their home was the game they learned to figure out very quickly. They mastered the environment by mimicking and enacting the rules of engagement. This process kept them connected to their family and a part of that critical community. Remember that human beings crave connection. So most of the time we do whatever we need to do to maintain it. This works out really well if we grow up in a healthy family, in a healthy environment, because the rules of engagement we learn are ones that help us to get our own needs met and to respect the needs of others.

What happens, though, if we grew up in a family where due to poverty, addiction, trauma, or other factors, the rules of engagement were not healthy ones? We still learn the rules in an expert manner. But we may find when we get outside of that insulated family environment that those ways of being don't actually help us to keep people close to us like they did in our family. In fact, we might find those same things that worked so well in our family actually seem to push other people away and cause repeated conflict in our relationships. So we've been playing basketball this whole time, and someone changed the game to soccer! What an unnerving experience, to realize the skills you have been mastering your whole life are not actually the ones that will help you get what you want. How frightening it must be to realize you actually don't know what you're doing and you might not even really know what you want or need in your life. This moment of realization is often what brings people into therapy—they develop a keen awareness that the way they have been doing things just isn't working anymore, and it feels horrible.

In this moment, I find it immensely helpful to remind people that if they learned the rules of a game once, they can learn new rules! This awareness though, that the cause of their problems might be a case of using the wrong rules for a new game, is the start of a powerful healing process. People are learners by design, and when we have the freedom to do so, we grow and evolve because that is how we were made! As believers, we can take solace in the fact that God knows and loves our innermost parts. Remember Psalm 139:13-16:

> For it was you who formed my inward parts;
> you knit me together in my mother's womb.
> I praise you, for I am fearfully and wonderfully made.
> Wonderful are your works;
> that I know very well.
> My frame was not hidden from you,
> when I was being made in secret,
> intricately woven in the depths of the earth.
> Your eyes beheld my unformed substance.
> In your book were written
> all the days that were formed for me,
> when none of them as yet existed.

This passage reminds us that there is no edge of our existence that God is not interested in healing. It is an exhortation that in our original formation, God's intentions were good and holy. Because we are made in God's image, we are wonderful in God's sight. At the core of who we are, no matter what we have been through, no matter how many mistakes we have made, no matter what the potential diagnosis is, we have the capacity to heal. The church, the well, is one of the ways we access the healing power of Jesus, and it is the hub of communication where we can get directed to the other resources we need to be whole. Ultimately, space at the well is about acknowledging that all of us, regardless of our identities, circumstances, life history, or emotional expression, are made in the image of God and are thus deserving of a prime spot in the community of believers. We all belong here, and we all need access to the well!

I hope you have found this book informative and helpful, and that it is a starting point for transformative ministry for mental health wherever you serve! I've included as an appendix a worship litany that could introduce your church to a renewed value around ministry for mental health. I want to close our time together with a prayer:

Lord Jesus, help us to exemplify you in all that we say and do. Help us to be the hands and feet of God as we seek to see each other, love each other, and provide opportunities for wholeness in your church. Help us to make space at the well of life by bearing witness to and honoring you in all those we encounter. Free us from the cultural and societal burdens that entice us to restrict access to the well of your living water. Amen.

Notes
1. Ronald T. Hyman. "Multiple Functions of Wells in the Tanakh," *Jewish Bible Quarterly* 34, no 3 (2006): 1.
2. Hyman, 4–5.
3. Hyman, 1.

A Litany to Affirm Ministry for Mental Health

Leader: "Before I formed you in the womb I knew you, and before you were born I consecrated you." (Jeremiah 1:5)

Congregation: Wise God, thank you for knowing and loving all of who we are. Help us to remember the gift of our personhood and to honor the personhood of others. Help us to make space for people to bring their full selves to the place of worship for healing and restoration.

Leader: "Come to me, all you that are weary and are carrying heavy burdens, and I will give you rest. Take my yoke upon you, and learn from me; for I am gentle and humble in heart, and you will find rest for your souls. For my yoke is easy, and my burden is light." (Matthew 11:28-30)

Congregation: Merciful God, remind us that you desire that we bring our burdens to you for help and healing. Let us be a congregation where burdens are shared and rest is granted. Help us to strive for mental and emotional health in the way that we seek spiritual health.

Leader: "Two are better than one, because they have a good reward for their toil. For if they fall, one will lift up the other; but woe to one who is alone and falls and does not have another to help." (Ecclesiastes 4:9-10)

Congregation: Loving God, help us to remember our commitment to love and support each other. Help us to show genuine care and to build strong relationships. Help those relationships to be conduits of healing for all of us.

Leader: "And let people learn to devote themselves to good works in order to meet urgent needs, so that they may not be unproductive." (Titus 3:14)

Congregation: Provider God, remind us that whatever we need, we can bring it to you. Help us to be your hands and feet by working to help address challenges in this church and in the community at large. Help us to be prepared to do good in your name and for your sake. Help us to recognize the gifts of the professionals you have equipped to lead us to health and wholeness.

Leader: "God is our refuge and strength, an ever-present help in trouble." (Psalm 46:1)

Congregation: Protecting God, remind us that no crisis is too big for you. Help us to see your movement in the actions of people who are called to serve you. Help us to turn to you for wisdom when we feel overwhelmed or unsure.

Leader: "My mouth will tell of your righteous acts, of your deeds of salvation all day long, though their number is past my knowledge. I will come praising the mighty deeds of the Lord GOD, I will praise your righteousness, yours alone." (Psalm 71:15-16)

Congregation: Redeeming God, we vow to testify of your goodness and healing power. Help us to tell our stories so that others may know and come to you.

All: Lord, make this space a living well from which all can drink. Help us to be a community where all can come and be healed. Help us to share the good news of Jesus, who saves, transforms, and delivers. Amen.

A Brief Primer on Common Mental Disorders

For a couple of reasons, I won't go into the detailed criteria for specific disorders in this appendix. First, our job as the church is not to diagnose people. That is the job of licensed and credentialed mental health professionals. Second, the strategies and tools presented in this book can be executed regardless of whether a person has a diagnosis or no matter what that diagnosis is. Still, you might hear a person mention that they have been diagnosed with a condition, and it could be helpful for you to have a sense of what that diagnosis means so you can understand their experience more thoroughly. The pages that follow will give you the broad strokes for the most common kinds of disorders. The descriptions are my casual-language interpretations of the diagnostic criteria from the *Diagnostic and Statistical Manual of Mental Disorders, 5th Edition (DSM-5)*, mixed with observations from my years of clinical experience. I will give particular attention to mental health symptoms that might show up intertwined with religious content and experiences. The descriptions are just a guide. If you have interest in the specific diagnostic criteria, please see the *DSM-5*.[1]

Anxiety disorders. Anxiety disorders can take on several different forms, but the main symptom is usually worry or fear. These emotions are either a reaction to past experiences or anticipatory stress about the future. A common disorder I see in my clinical practice is generalized anxiety disorder (GAD), which is marked by global, unproductive worry. Folks with this disorder cannot take in the "if you're going to pray, don't worry" admonition. As is common with many disorders, people with GAD often experience tension and pain in the neck, shoulders, and back. They have a hard time separating rational fears from irrational ones, and they spend an excessive amount of time worrying about a large number of things.

Though it is not as common as GAD, obsessive-compulsive disorder (OCD) is marked by obsessive irrational thoughts about things such as cleanliness, order, or safety. One type of obsession can also be religious in nature and related to being excessively concerned about sinfulness or moral unworthiness. This form of OCD with excessive attention to religious content is called "scrupulosity."[2] Scrupulosity is marked by a pattern of literal or extreme interpretation of Scriptures, excessive concerns about engaging in blasphemous or sacrilegious acts, and long periods of time spent engaging in spiritual rituals beyond what is the norm in the particular religious tradition. Some authors even suggest that certain religious leaders like Martin Luther exhibited scrupulosity.[3] Scrupulosity can easily be misinterpreted as piousness or an extreme commitment to a faith walk. However, a key discerning feature is that people with OCD experience intense anxiety in response to these uncontrollable excessive thoughts. They engage in compulsions as a way to manage anxiety-provoking thoughts. These compulsions include repetitive acts or behaviors such as hand washing, tapping, checking, or in the case of scrupulosity, praying or other religious rituals. When people with these disorders are unable to engage in these behaviors, they experience intense anxiety and emotional or physical dysregulation.

Another anxiety disorder that might be likely to come up, particularly when it comes to people participating in worship or other church activities, is social phobia or social anxiety. This disorder is marked by intense worry about being embarrassed or ridiculed in public and is often activated around activities such as speaking in public, performing in front of large groups of people, or sometimes even being in crowds where the attention could possibly be on the person with social phobia. As you can imagine, this might show up as excessive wariness about tasks like reading Scripture during worship, speaking in front of the congregation, and the like. Social anxiety can be confusing for people who do not have the disorder, because the person often appears to be competent and successful. They might not experience anxiety in other domains of their lives and be otherwise well-adjusted. Still, the thought of being in front of others brings terror and will likely lead to avoidance of these assigned tasks. Work to be respectful of the person's fears, even if you think they are unreasonable. Ask if there is anything you can do to support them or to help them manage the fear. This may include practicing what they will say a number of times, having someone go up to the pulpit with them, or offering other support.

Bipolar disorders. Bipolar disorders are marked by instability in mood. People with this family of disorders experience a combination of elevated mood and depressed mood, often with little transitional time in between. During depressive periods, people with these disorders look and behave like people with depressive disorders. During periods of high mood, called mania or hypomania, people seem to be excessively happy, talkative, restless, even to the point of irritability. Often people will experience what we call grandiosity, which is when they overestimate their ability to perform a large or extensive task or view themselves as overly important. People experiencing mania tend to engage in risky behaviors such as unsafe sex, excessive drug use, or overspending. Because they may also experience psychosis, they often end up in hospitals because they can easily become a danger to themselves.

It is not uncommon for psychosis to be religious in content. I can recall several clients who had strong beliefs that God was telling them to make major life changes, run away from home, or take some other drastic measure. A key way we distinguish this disorder from someone receiving a revelation from God in a nonpsychotic sense is that people with mental illness often demonstrate pressured speech, irritability, or unwillingness to consider the risks and possible consequences of engaging in drastic actions. A major challenge with bipolar disorders is medication compliance. Because mania can be fun for people, sometimes they miss that high when they are on the appropriate medication. Thus, a crucial pastoral care role is to work to ensure these people take their medications regularly.

Depressive disorders. When people have depressive disorders, they generally present with the primary symptom of sadness. In addition to sadness, they may experience changes in appetite, sleep, energy level, and ability to concentrate. People with severe depression often report feelings of worthlessness, helplessness, and hopelessness, and may report feelings of wanting to die. Others may isolate themselves, withdraw, or even instigate conflicts in close friendships or relationships. They may appear to be overly sensitive, tearful, and emotionally overwhelmed. Many people report not being interested or engaged in things they would normally enjoy. Black folks, and ethnic minorities in general, tend to engage in what mental health professionals call somatization, which is a tendency to experience emotional distress as physical symptoms. People who are depressed might experience headaches, unexplained aches and pains, and/or heaviness or restlessness in the body. Depression also interacts with physical conditions such as thyroid disease and diabetes, which are common in the black community. Probably the most commonly diagnosed depressive disorder in adults is major depressive disorder.

Psychotic and delusional disorders. These are rarer but are particularly dangerous disorders due to the level of impairment. People with these disorders have a central struggle related to an inability to distinguish between what is real and what is not real. The challenge of dealing with these disorders, in contrast to the disorders discussed above, is that people who are psychotic might not be aware that they are out of touch with reality or are behaving in strange ways. The most common symptom is auditory hallucinations—hearing voices. People in this category might also experience erratic or unusual emotional responses, difficulty with memory or speech, and strange behaviors. Of all the disorders we've discussed, people with psychotic disorders are most likely to be the ones who "seem" to have something wrong and need help urgently. People can also have other psychotic experiences involving smells, tactile sensations, or even tastes. As we discussed earlier, any sign of possible psychosis warrants an urgent referral to a medical professional.

A challenge in this particular area is that our belief system affirms a belief in things we cannot see. We discuss hearing the voice of God, seeing visions, and believing in the miraculous. So determining whether something is a spiritual experience or a psychotic episode is not always clear-cut. Often people with true psychotic disorders will show deterioration in other ways, especially in speech, memory, and motor function. Their conversation might demonstrate what we call "loose associations," where the content of what they're talking about does not seem to be coherent. Look for all the signs you can that the person's experience is broader than just a religious one. The most known form of psychotic disorder is schizophrenia, but there are other slight variations. One I have seen come up a lot in community mental health is schizoaffective disorder, which is a combination of psychotic symptoms and mood symptoms.

Further complicating the distinction between psychosis and religious experiences is delusional disorder. In contrast to the pervasive impairment we often see with psychotic disorders, people with delusional disorder have one major symptom with little other impairment—delusions. Delusions are bizarre, irrational beliefs that are not based in reality but are strongly held. Some common forms of delusions are thought insertion (belief that others are putting thoughts into one's head or controlling one's behavior), persecutory (belief that others are trying to cause a person hurt or harm), or erotomanic (belief that a person is in love with the delusional person when there is no evidence for this). Religious delusions can incorporate things such as believing God is communicating with the delusional person through a specific method (the radio, words in a book, images on the TV), that one is on a special mission from God that other people are not privy to, or other related beliefs. You can see how these might be difficult to distinguish from actual spiritual or religious phenomena. As a matter of fact, there is some evidence that suggests people who are highly engaged in religious activity when they become psychotic are more likely to have severer religious delusions and higher frequency of those delusions.[4] As far as what we can do in the church, if there's any doubt about whether the person seems to be in touch with reality or if they are experiencing significant problems managing their lives, it is best to get a professional referral lined up.

Substance-use disorders. Substance-use disorders encompass a broad range of symptoms that result from the overuse of a substance. Keeping in mind that people can have a substance use disorder when using either a legal or illegal substance is important. We might be tempted to pay less attention to legal substance use, such as excessive alcohol consumption or the use of prescription drugs, but these behaviors can lead to an addictive process if unchecked. Regardless of the substance, people with substance use disorders demonstrate a common constellation of symptoms. Substance use becomes an addictive process when the reward system in the brain is activated in such a way that people become less able to make reasonable decisions about their substance use and start to neglect everyday activities to obtain, use, or recover from the substance. People with these disorders experience significant problems from their use—family and relational conflicts, legal or job-related problems, and even financial problems. However, these problems do not deter them from using. Often, this can be due to psychological or even physical dependence on the substance to function with some semblance of normalcy.

Because substance use drastically changes the brain, people with substance use disorders have intense cravings, withdrawal when not using the substance, and high rates of relapse. Note that substance use disorders are highly genetic in nature, meaning the risk for substance dependence is much greater for those who have a family member who has struggled with addiction. It is crucial to emphasize here that addiction is not a moral failing. It is not as simple as making a decision not to use. By the time people are engaged in an addictive process, changes to the brain have physically or neurologically impaired their ability to make decisions and understand the consequences of their behavior. This does not mean we don't hold people accountable for their actions, but it does mean we must pair that accountability with invitations to engage in treatment and be provided support in the community. If people with addictions could stop on their own, they would!

Trauma-related disorders. These are probably best known in the context of post-traumatic stress disorder (PTSD). People tend to think about PTSD as being a fear- or panic-based response to a major horrifying or life-threatening event. We tend to think of PTSD in relation to experiences such as war, car accidents, sexual assaults, or other drastic events. While these are certainly possibilities, trauma-related disorders might be more likely to be seen in the context of the church in a more hidden or nuanced way. Lots of definitions of trauma get thrown around, but the one I like to use in my therapy practice is this one: *a boundary violation or crossing that disturbs one's sense of safety.* A simpler way to say this is, things either happened that weren't supposed to happen, or didn't happen that were supposed to happen, and this course of events led to the person feeling a lack of security in the world around them. When we use this definition, there are many more things that are considered traumatic events—parental abuse or neglect, poverty, repeated rejection or ostracization, and the list goes on.

People react to trauma in a number of ways, including fear, anger, irritability, and social or emotional disengagement. Trauma survivors often protect against a future violation by steeling themselves and building a wall to keep others out of their lives. They may interpret harmless words and actions as threatening or aggressive in some way. They might also attach intensely and quickly to people whom they deem as safe, but later be disappointed when these people don't live up to their expectations. Many folks who have experienced trauma have strong beliefs that the world is unsafe, that all people will eventually hurt them, or that certain groups of people can't be trusted. These are the people who might be most resistant to the goal of persistent presence we talked about in chapter 2. At the same time, they are the people who are in most desperate need of our love and support. They need us to be gentle and unwavering despite their attempts to push us away.

In my clinical practice, I see a common theme of black clients coming in and talking about traumatic events but not labeling them as such. There are a variety of reasons for this. First, as we have been discussing throughout the book, black folks as a cultural group have experienced some heinous things, particularly in this country. With the historical backdrop of chattel slavery, having parents who fought all the time doesn't seem like much of a complaint.

Authors such as Joy DeGruy[5] and Stacey Patton[6] have discussed how the cultural and historical context of black folks in America even shapes the way we talk to our children about how to make sense of the negative events that happen in their lives and how our difficulty naming our pain can lead to a host of problems in every domain of life. Early messages to children to "suck it up" or "be strong" without allowing them to understand and express how negative events have impacted them are a recipe for undercover trauma responses later in life. My simple recommendation for this complex problem is this: we must call a thing a thing! A blood relationship does not absolve anyone's responsibility to treat a family member with love and respect. Just because a family has dealt with an issue for generations doesn't mean that they are not impacted by it. What we name and pray against in the church as "generational curses" is something mental health professionals recognize as "generational trauma." When we don't call it what it is and work to heal it, that trauma gets passed down just like a gene.

The final two disorders I will discuss are often diagnosed in childhood, and they are particularly relevant as we think about how the youth in our churches interact with educational and other community-based systems: *attention deficit/hyperactivity disorder* (ADHD) and *oppositional defiant disorder* (ODD). A common refrain in the black community is that our children are overdiagnosed with ADHD. In fact, research suggests that black kids are underdiagnosed.[7] A variety of cultural factors can lead to this reality, including a lack of resources in schools, racial bias, and socioeconomic status. Stigma also rears its ugly head, as black parents might be hesitant or delayed in seeking out services if they have a concern about their child's academic performance. The real concern with inappropriate diagnosis for black kids is that children might not be able to live up to their full academic potential because they are not getting the appropriate resources and support. As we know, poor educational experiences put people at risk for a host of other problems later in life.

So what is ADHD? It is a disorder that leads to difficulty managing and directing attention. In children it can show up as difficulty paying attention or following directions, difficulty completing complex tasks, making careless mistakes, and difficulty staying seated or quiet. One important feature that distinguishes ADHD from other school-based problems is that these behaviors show up across domains, not just at school. If a child truly has ADHD, these behaviors will show up at church too! If you do see symptoms, it's important for parents to seek out support. While medications are often recommended for ADHD, they are not required. Parents should know there are other options for working with children so that they can adjust to the challenges brought by ADHD and receive appropriate accommodations.

Oppositional defiant disorder is another disorder that is likely to be diagnosed in childhood if at all. It is marked by refusal to heed the requests of authority, persistent violation of the social contract in a community, defiance, irritability, vindictiveness, and disrespect. Unlike ADHD, ODD can be confined to one domain, like home or school. Because of what we might be likely to call "attitude problems," people with ODD are likely to have great difficulty in their relationships, particularly those with parents and teachers but with peers as well. At a cognitive and emotional level, kids with ODD often see threat where others do not. For instance, they might interpret a person greeting them in a joking manner as some form of interpersonal challenge. They are often on high alert for conflict and feel that the demands placed on them in their environment are unreasonable or too great.

Significant evidence exists that suggests ODD is strongly associated with trauma and parental neglect or abuse.[8] Thus, what we might see as oppositional behaviors might actually be a trauma response in disguise. If this is the case, then these kids probably need exactly the opposite of what they put out into the world. They need to feel safe, loved, and supported, even while they are pushing people away. Research suggests that both ADHD and ODD are likely to be comorbid, or co-occuring, with other mental health conditions such as depression and anxiety.[9] In addition, these children are at much greater risk for experiencing mental health problems as adults. The bottom line is that children who are diagnosed with a mental health condition, and their families, need all the support the church has to offer. Childhood is a crucial time that shapes the adults we become. Children, just like any other parishioner, need space at the well to talk about their concerns and to get their needs met.

# Appendix B

Though understanding these disorders can be a helpful frame, there are a host of other behaviors that might be dysfunctional or unhealthy but that may not fit neatly into a diagnostic category. Whether or not we know what to call it, what we do know is to work the model: make space at the well. Be like Jesus.

Notes

1. *Diagnostic and Statistical Manual of Mental Disorders: DSM-5* (Arlington, VA: American Psychiatric Publishing, 2013).

2. John P. Dehlin, Kate L. Morrison, and Michael P. Twohig, "Acceptance and Commitment Therapy as a Treatment for Scrupulosity in Obsessive Compulsive Disorder," *Behavior Modification* 37, no. 3 (2013): 409–30, https://doi.org/10.1177/0145445512475134.

3. Paul Cefalu, "The Doubting Disease: Religious Scrupulosity and Obsessive-Compulsive Disorder in Historical Context," *Journal of Medical Humanities* 31, no. 2 (2010): 111–25, https://doi.org/10.1007/s10912-010-9107-3.

4. Glen E. Getz, David E. Fleck, and Stephen M. Strakowski, "Frequency and Severity of Religious Delusions in Christian Patients with Psychosis," *Psychiatry Research* 103, no. 1 (2001): 87–91, https://doi.org/10.1016/s0165-1781(01)00262-1.

5. Joy DeGruy Leary, *Post Traumatic Slave Syndrome: America's Legacy of Enduring Injury and Healing: The Study Guide* (Portland, OR: Joy DeGruy Publications, 2009).

6. Stacey L. Patton, *Spare the Kids: Why Whupping Children Won't Save Black America* (Boston: Beacon, 2017).

7. Myles D. Moody, "'Us Against Them': Schools, Families, and the Diagnosis of ADHD among Black Children," *Journal of Racial and Ethnic Health Disparities* 4, no. 5 (2016): 949–56, https://doi.org/10.1007/s40615-016-0298-9.

8. *DSM-5.*

9. M. K. Nock, I. Hwang, N. A. Sampson, and R. C. Kessler, "Mental Disorders, Comorbidity and Suicidal Behavior: Results from the National Comorbidity Survey Replication," *Molecular Psychiatry* 15, no. 8 (2009): 868–76, https://doi.org/doi:10.1038/mp.2009.29.

Bibliography

American Foundation for Suicide Prevention. "Suicide Statistics." AFSP. April 16, 2019. https://afsp.org/about-suicide/sui cide-statistics/.

Betancourt, Joseph R., Alexander R. Green, J. Emilio Carrillo, and Elyse R. Park. "Cultural Competence and Health Care Disparities: Key Perspectives and Trends." *Health Affairs* 24, no. 2 (2005): 499–505.

"Black and African American Communities and Mental Health." *Mental Health America.* Last modified November 6, 2013. http://www.mentalhealthamerica.net/african-american-men-tal-health.

Blank, Michael B., Marcus Mahmood, Jeanne C. Fox, and Thomas Guterbock. "Alternative Mental Health Services: The Role of the Black Church in the South." *American Journal of Public Health* 92, no 10 (October 2002). https://doi.org/10.2105/ AJPH.92.10.1668.

Brandt, Allen M. "Racism and Research: The Case of the Tuskegee Syphilis Study." *Hastings Center Report* 8, no. 9 (1978): 21–29. https://dash.harvard.edu/handle/1/3372911.

Brown, Jessica Young, and Micah L. McCreary. "Pastors' Counseling Practices and Perceptions of Mental Health Services." *Journal of Pastoral Care and Counseling,* 68, no. 1 (2014): 1–14.

Cefalu, Paul. "The Doubting Disease: Religious Scrupulosity and Obsessive-Compulsive Disorder in Historical Context." *Journal of Medical Humanities* 31, no. 2 (2010): 111–25. https://doi.org/ 10.1007/s10912-010-9107-3.

Brown, Jessica Young. "More Than a Prayer: Pastors' Perceptions of Mental Health Services." (2010).

Centers for Disease Control and Prevention. "Intimate Partner Violence: Prevention Strategies." Accessed November 5, 2019. www.cdc.gov/violenceprevention/intimatepartnerviolence/preven tion.html.

Dehlin, John P., Kate L. Morrison, and Michael P. Twohig. "Acceptance and Commitment Therapy as a Treatment for Scrupulosity in Obsessive Compulsive Disorder." *Behavior Modification* 37, no. 3 (2013): 409–30. https://doi.org/10.1177/0145445512475134.

Dempsey, Keith, S. Kent Butler, and LaTrece Gaither. "Black Churches and Mental Health Professionals: Can This Collaboration Work?" *Journal of Black Studies* 47, no. 1 (2016): 73–87. https://doi.org/10.1177/0021934715613588.

Diagnostic and Statistical Manual of Mental Disorders: DSM-5. Arlington, VA: American Psychiatric Publishing, 2013.

Forum for Theological Exploration. "The FTE Guide to VocationCARE." 2012. https://fteleaders.org/uploads/files/GUIDE %20TO%20VOCATIONCARE%202012%20Low.pdf.

Getz, Glen E., David E. Fleck, and Stephen M. Strakowski. "Frequency and Severity of Religious Delusions in Christian Patients with Psychosis." *Psychiatry Research* 103, no. 1 (2001): 87–91. https://doi.org/10.1016/s0165-1781(01)00262-1.

Gilkes, Cheryl Townsend. "The Black Church as a Therapeutic Community: Suggested Areas for Research into the Black Religious Experience." *Journal of the Interdenominational Theological Center* 8, no. 1 (1980). http://digitalcommons.auctr.edu/itcj/vol8/iss1/8.

Griffith, Ezra E. H., John L. Young, and Dorothy L. Smith. "An Analysis of the Therapeutic Elements in a Black Church Service." *Psychiatric Services* 35, no. 5 (1984): 464–69. https://doi.org/10.1176/ps.35.5.464.

Guzik, David. "John Chapter 4." Enduring Word. November 5, 2019. https://enduringword.com/bible-commentary/john-4/.

Harrelson, Walter. *The New Interpreter's Study Bible*. Nashville: Abingdon, 2003, John 4:1-15.

Hyman, Ronald T. "Multiple Functions of Wells in the Tanakh." *Jewish Bible Quarterly* 34, no. 3 (2006): 1–10.

Kearney, Chris, and Timothy Trull. *Abnormal Psychology and Life: A Dimensional Approach*, 2nd ed., 16. Belmont, CA: Cengage Learning, 2015.

"Laws in Your State." RAINN. www.rainn.org.

Leary, Joy DeGruy. *Post Traumatic Slave Syndrome: America's Legacy of Enduring Injury and Healing: The Study Guide*. Portland, OR: Joy DeGruy Publications, 2009.

Maslow, Abraham H. *The Psychology of Science: A Reconnaissance*. New York: Harper and Row, 1974.

Mental Health First Aid. "Find a Mental Health First Aid Course." October 18, 2013. https://www.mentalhealthfirstaid.org/take-a-course/find-a-course/.

Merriam-Webster. s.v. "stigma." Accessed September 13, 2018. https://www.merriam-webster.com/dictionary/stigma.

Moody, Myles D. "Us Against Them": Schools, Families, and the Diagnosis of ADHD among Black Children." *Journal of Racial and Ethnic Health Disparities* 4, no. 5 (2016): 949–56. https://doi.org/10.1007/s40615-016-0298-9.

National Alliance on Mental Illness. "Mental Health by the Numbers." NAMI. Accessed January 2, 2019. https://www.nami.org/learn-more/mental-health-by-the-numbers.

National Alliance on Mental Illness. "Mental Health Month." NAMI. Accessed May 18, 2019. https://www.nami.org/mentalhealthmonth.

New York Public Library and Schomburg Center for Research in Black Culture. *The New York Public Library African American Desk Reference*. New York: Wiley & Sons, 1999.

Nock, M. K., I. Hwang, N. A. Sampson, and R. C. Kessler. "Mental Disorders, Comorbidity and Suicidal Behavior: Results from the National Comorbidity Survey Replication." *Molecular Psychiatry* 15, no. 8 (2009): 868–76. https://doi.org/10.1038/mp.2009.29.

Patton, Stacey L. *Spare the Kids: Why Whupping Children Won't Save Black America.* Boston: Beacon, 2017.

Quinette, Paul. "Gatekeeper: Suicide Prevention Training." *PsycEXTRA Dataset,* January 2007, 1–38. https://doi.org/10.1037/e537222009-001.

Substance Abuse and Mental Health Services Administration. *Key Substance Use and Mental Health Indicators in the United States: Results from the 2017 National Survey on Drug Use and Health.* HHS Publication No. SMA 18-5068, NSDUH Series H-53. Rockville, MD: Center for Behavioral Health Statistics and Quality, Substance Abuse and Mental Health Services Administration. https://www.samhsa.gov/data/sites/default/files/cbhsq-reports/NSDUHFFR2017/NSDUHFFR2017.pdf.

Unger, Merrill F. *The New Unger's Bible Dictionary.* Chicago: Moody, 1966, s.v., "well."

Woodson, Carter G. *The History of the Negro Church.* Washington, DC: Associated Publishers, 1979.

Index

A
active listening, 31
ADHD (attention deficit/
  hyperactivity disorder),
  101–102
adolescents, disorders of, 52,
  101–102
Alabama, Tuskegee Syphilis
  Study and, 2
alcohol, 59
altar, 81
anxiety disorders, 93–95
asexuals, ministry to, 80–81
assault, 56–57
attention deficit/hyperactivity
  disorder (ADHD), 101–102
auditory hallucinations, 96–97
authentic relationships, 17–18

B
behaviors
  changes within, 50–51
  development of, 19
  irrational, 43
  repetitive, 94
  responses to, 51
  risky, 43, 95
beliefs, unusual, 41, 57–59

bereavement, 10–11, 29–30
bipolar disorders, 95–96
bisexuals, ministry to, 80–81
black church, history of, xii,
  xiii–xiv
brain, substance abuse and,
  98–99
burdens, bearing of, 7–8

C
campfires, xiii
caregivers, 78
children, disorders of, 101–102
church
  closed environment of, 25
  culture and, 81–82
  hierarchal structure of,
    55–56
  mission of, 22–23, 76, 77
  prayer and praise service,
    63–64, 71
  relationships within, 17–18
  resources of, 85
  response from, 29–30
  role of, 19–21, 86, 88
  sexual orientation and,
    80–81
  as social community, 16

Index

Index

O

obsessive-compulsive disorder (OCD), 94
oppositional defiant disorder (ODD), 101–102
overcoming process, xiv

P

panic, 43
pastoral care, x, 42–43
pastors, role of, 4–5
Patton, Stacey, 100
persecutory belief, 97
persistence, 25–26
personality, 50–51
Pharaoh, story of, 47–48
physical assault, 56–57
post-traumatic stress disorder (PTSD), 99
poverty, 4
prayer, 4–5, 6, 17, 90–92
prayer and praise service, 63–64, 71
preparation, 48, 60–61
prescription drugs, 59, 98–99
problem-solving mode, 32
psychosis, 95–96
psychotic disorder, 41, 57–59, 96–98
PTSD (post-traumatic stress disorder), 99

Q

queers, ministry to, 80–81
Question, Persuade, Refer (QPR), 53–54

R

reaping, 77–78
referrals, 37–43
reflection, 33, 45
rejection, 11–12
relationships, 17–18, 25–26, 55–57
religious delusions, 97–98
reporting laws, 57
resources, 37–38, 48–50, 85
responses, 34

S

sadness, 96
Samaritan woman, xvi–xvii, 11, 24–25, 44–45, 60–61, 72–73, 77
SAMHSA (Substance Abuse and Mental Health Services Administration), 9–10
schizophrenia, 97
Scripture, misinterpretation of, 65
scrupulosity, 94
self-denial, xiv–xv
sensory experiences, unusual, 41, 57–59

sexual orientation, ministry and, 80–81
slavery, xii–xiii
social anxiety, 94–95
social phobia, 94–95
Solomon, story of, 66
sowing, 77–78
space, structural readiness and, 36
stigma, 1, 6–7, 76
structural readiness, 35–40, 46
submission, 55–56
substance abuse, 41, 43, 49, 59
Substance Abuse and Mental Health Services Administration (SAMHSA), 9–10
substance use disorders, 98–99
suffering, 7, 12, 68–69
suicidal ideation, 52–55
suicide, 40–41, 49, 52, 80–81
symptoms, mental health, 10, 43
syphilis, 2

T
tent meetings, xiii
testimonies, 63–64, 71, 72–74
therapists, 37–39
thyroid disease, 96
tracking, process of, 36–37
transference of trust, 39, 46
trauma, 99, 102

trauma-related disorders, 99–101
Tuskegee Syphilis Study, 2

U
unconditional love, 18
United States Department of Health, Education, and Welfare, 2

V
village, church as, 16
voices, hearing of, 57–59, 96–97

W
well, significance of, xv–xvi, 81–83
women, domestic violence and, 55–56
worry, 43, 93